THE ENGAGED GROOM

Collins

An Imprint of HarperCollinsPublishers

You're Getting Married.

THE

ENGAGED

GROOM

Read This Book.

Doug Gordon

HarperCollins books may be purchased for educational,
business, or sales promotional use. For information, please
write: Special Markets Department, HarperCollins Publishers,
10 East 53rd Street, New York, NY 10022.

FIRST EDITION

Designed by Jennifer Ann Daddio

Illustrated by Alexis Seabrook

Library of Congress Cataloging-in-Publication Data
has been applied for.

ISBN-10: 0-06-085582-7
ISBN-13: 978-0-06-085582-6

06 07 08 09 10 WBC/RRD 10 9 8 7 6 5 4 3 2 1

Contents

Part Two
THE FINER POINTS 83

Part Three
TAKING A BREAK . . . SORT OF 169

Part Four
THE FINAL COUNTDOWN 193

WHAT IS AN ENGAGED GROOM?

Hath not a groom taste?
Hath not a groom senses,
Preferences, passions?
Subject to the same demanding family as a bride is?
If you ignore us, do we not grow resentful?
And if you lose us in Bloomingdale's,
Do we not head straight for the electronics department?

—NOT SHAKESPEARE

Planning a wedding is a massive undertaking, a task that has traditionally been the exclusive province of a bride and her mother. In years past, most grooms' responsibilities ended immediately following the proposal. Having exhausted most of his energy shopping for a ring and picking the perfect place to pop the question, the groom was largely expected to stand on the sidelines. Except for the token appearance at an engagement party or a shower, making an appointment to get his tux fitted, and figuring out where to go on a honeymoon, the traditional groom wasn't expected to do much of anything at all. The wedding industry historically viewed grooms as almost an afterthought. Even when a groom did have a preference about cake flavors or invitation styles, his bride and mother-in-law-to-be humored him with a polite nod and then made their own choices anyway.

You are reading this book, I suppose, because you are a different type of groom. Despite a wedding industry that largely caters to the fairy-tale fantasies of women and ignores 50 percent of wedding participants, you *want* to be involved. You're not content to just lick envelopes and run errands for your bride; you want to be a full-fledged partner making decisions *with* your bride. While you may not put your foot down on every decision and you know when you're out of your league, you believe that a groom's responsibilities should go beyond the three "sh's": showering, shaving, and showing up. *You are an Engaged Groom.*

You might be more involved with the wedding planning for a purely practical reason. These days, it's probably not possible for your fiancée to do everything herself. As a professional woman with precious little time on her hands, she's as entitled to take a break from it all as you are. After a long day at work, she might not feel like taking on the lion's share of the planning. Even if you aren't initially inclined to be so involved, you might find that circumstance forces you to track down a caterer or negotiate the price of a deposit with a bandleader.

There is another reason why men are becoming more involved, one cynically and coldly detached from romantic notions of love, commitment, and a lifelong partnership. And that, of course, is money. With couples getting married later in life today than they might have a generation ago, many brides and grooms are well entrenched in their careers, possibly with advanced degrees and advanced salaries. Twenty- and thirtysomethings who already know the finer points of compensation packages, mortgages, and investment portfolios might feel a little strange taking money from their parents. While a groom's future in-laws might still pay much of the wedding expenses, if he's the one who's writing the check to cover the band's fee, he'll probably have more leeway to tell them what music to play.

As guys take a more active role in planning their weddings, they can inject a dose of sanity into what is increasingly becoming an insane endeavor. Average wedding budgets are spinning out of control and are on track to exceed the cost of a luxury automobile or a semester at a private university. Why? It's not because some committee of formal-wearing wedding elders sits on high and dictates that every wedding must cost more than the down payment on a two-bedroom apartment. It's because the wedding industry has expanded to the point where even the most well-meaning bride can find herself inundated with an incredible amount of choices. Faced with an industry that scares a lot of women into believing that if they don't do everything according to what they read in magazines and on the Internet, then they'll have the worst wedding in the history of marriage, many brides become paralyzed to the point of being unable to say no to even the most outrageous wedding-related goods and services. From the stationers who sell scented ink for labeling invitations to the fashion consultants who push jewel-encrusted tiaras, the choices in planning a wedding can be overwhelming.

That men have been so distant from wedding planning for so long allows them to be properly distant when what is most lacking in the wedding industry is any sense of perspective. Of course a wedding day is important, but no one needs to go insane—or bankrupt—trying to plan the perfect wedding. I'd hate to fall into the trap of stereotyping anyone, but the very fact that the wedding industry has long ignored grooms has created the perfect opportunity for men everywhere to call its bluff. Scented ink? Come on.

But that's not to say that an Engaged Groom only gets involved to dismiss other people's wishes or doesn't get a little carried away himself sometimes. On the contrary, an Engaged Groom steps up to the plate precisely because his wedding is important to him, at least as a reflection of his love for his hopefully equally Engaged Bride. If you go through the entire wedding planning without ever being expected to take any sort of active role, how much of a role will you take in your marriage? Today's modern, more egalitarian relationships require an Engaged Groom to offer if not an equal splitting of the wedding planning duties, then at least a full commitment to doing his part. And even the most sensitive, best-intentioned groom can start to get obsessed over paper texture and china patterns after a while.

Not only are weddings becoming increasingly expensive for the people who throw them, but they also involve big financial commitments on the part of the people who attend them. Many guests have to spend a lot of money on airfare, hotels, tuxedo rentals, bridesmaids' dresses, and other expenses just to show up for the celebration. Yes, the focus at your wedding will always be on you and your fiancée, but you'll have a better time if your guests are having a good time, too. That doesn't mean that you have to have your wedding at the local VFW hall or host everyone at a highway motel so that no one has to spend a lot of money on transportation or lodging, but it does mean that you and your bride might think twice about having a destination wedding at a pricey resort or demanding that your groomsmen and bridesmaids wear expensive outfits.

As you plan your wedding, you'll probably hear the words *should* and *have to* used quite frequently. As in "You *should* have a fifteen-piece orchestra." "You *have to* get married on a Sunday at three." "You really *should* get candies printed with your initials to give to your guests." Baloney. The only thing you should do and, in fact, have to do is have a good time. How you and your bride decide to do that is up to the two of you. You don't have to have a bouquet toss if doing so will make your single friends feel uncomfortable. You don't have to serve a wedding cake if you're allergic to wheat. Do what makes you both feel comfortable. With the exception of certain religious rituals and civic requirements, few parts of a wedding ceremony and reception are etched in stone. While you may have to balance your strong opinions against the desires of your bride and her parents, everything can be up for a polite discussion, reinterpretation, or even exclusion.

WHAT TO LOOK FOR IN THIS BOOK

If you are looking for a complete wedding planning primer, it wouldn't hurt to read this book from beginning to end, but it's certainly not necessary. In fact, it may more accurately reflect your experience if you open the book to any random page to find answers to some of your more pressing questions. Putting all of the details of your wedding together can often feel like an ad hoc sort of process; there's no telling exactly what task will pop up when. So, if your first concern is picking a date, skip ahead to chapter three and then refer back to chapter two if you need some pointers on making a budget. If you're crunched for time and are worried about when your invitations should go out, find the answer in chapter nine. This book is designed so you can choose your own wedding adventure.

My goal is to help the Engaged Groom find areas where he can be involved, recognizing his talents, strengths, and weaknesses. You probably don't need anyone to tell you how to build a Web site or format an Excel spreadsheet, but you might not have thought that building a wedding Web site or making a budget are two ways for you to take an active role.

I'm also hoping that some of the book will help give voice to questions and concerns that many grooms share. With the kind of perspective that an Engaged Groom can bring to wedding planning, you may well be the only person who wonders about the need for monogrammed matchbooks when no one you know smokes. Nevertheless, even with an aversion to frivolous expenses, you might need a little help talking through your reasons.

To help you in your efforts, you'll find Engaged Groom Tips scattered throughout this book. Each one will offer you tips on saving money or time and calls into question a few long-standing wedding traditions that most people take for granted. Hopefully you'll find all or some of these helpful as you argue against having your wedding on a three-day weekend or tell your father why it will actually be okay for the birds if everyone throws rice at the end of your ceremony.

WHAT NOT TO LOOK FOR IN THIS BOOK

This book won't walk you through every step of wedding planning. You either already know where to get wedding invitations printed, know where to ask if you need to find a printer, or don't care at all and have left this job to your fiancée. Not knowing you and your bride, there's no way I could include sample menus to satisfy every palate or write a list of songs that can be played as members of your wedding party walk down the aisle. In some areas you'll just have to be on your own.

It's a defining characteristic of most grooms' guides to refer to well-meaning fellas as idiots, dummies, clueless oafs, or worse. Don't let anyone talk down to you. You are not a ticking time bomb of ineptitude waiting to ruin your bride's perfect day. You're not an idiot or a dummy if you've never thought about corkage fees or embossed invitations. You're simply a well-meaning, enthusiastic Engaged Groom. You're not an expert, and guess what? Having only gone through wedding planning once, neither am I. (People who have been married ten times rarely write books about wedding planning.)

Here are a few other things you won't find in this book:

Tips on how to buy an engagement ring. Even a guy with the biggest propensity for getting involved probably never gave much thought to his wedding before he got engaged, so I'm assuming you've already bought an engagement ring and proposed to your girlfriend. I'm also assuming she said yes. If not, why are you reading this book?

Any reference to bridezillas. Your fiancée is not a stereotype. She's a human being, and planning a party of this magnitude can make even the most steely-eyed bride cry if she wants to. It's okay if she needs to break down every once in a while. That's not to say that your fiancée won't get a little narrow-minded at times or lose sight of the bigger picture, but hopefully you have an open enough relationship to offer comfort when she needs it or to politely tell her when she needs to relax.

Tips on how to deal with a mother-in-law from hell. Since when do mothers-in-law have a monopoly on bad behavior? There is no one-size-fits-all approach to dealing with family, and only you will know how to deal with yours. Given the size of the average wedding and the shape of modern families, the person causing you the most drama could well be your father, sister-in-law, distant cousin, or fraternity brother. Consider the stereotype of the wicked-witch mother-in-law retired, at least as far as I'm concerned.

THE ENGAGED GROOM—
HOW TO BE ONE EVEN IF YOU AREN'T

The image of the little girl standing in front of a mirror pretending to be a bride when she grows up might be a stereotype, but how many boys dream at night of walking down the aisle to Pachelbel, Bach, or Handel? Even the most enlightened Renaissance man might be unsure exactly how he can get involved in wedding planning.

It might be easy for you to help with some aspects of the preparations. If you consider yourself a budding Emeril and love to cook, but your fiancée hates to boil water, you might find yourself in meetings and on the phone with the caterer and picking out the pots and pans on your registry. But if you don't have the faintest idea or care about bed linens and flowers, it's okay to leave some trips to the department store to your bride.

If you are at a total loss as to how to get involved, dip your toes in the shallow end of the wedding pool with these jobs to test the wedding waters:

- **Producer.** Even if you've never given much thought to your wedding, you can still create budgets, make lists, and take a big-picture role while your fiancée covers some of the day-to-day decisions. In *Your Wedding: The Movie,* your bride is essentially the director and you're the producer.

- **IT consultant.** Use simple computer software to create spreadsheets for tracking addresses, RSVPs, and who has been sent a thank-you note. If you are Web-savvy, volunteer to build a personalized wedding Web site where guests can find important information about your wedding.
- **Delivery guy.** You won't need brown shorts for this job, but wherever you can lend a hand with the logistical effort of putting together an event of this magnitude, do so. Pick up your invitations at the printer's. Drop them off at the post office. Your bride will have more time to focus on what's important to her and will appreciate your effort.
- **DJ.** You carry an MP3 player everywhere and spend more money on music than some people spend on food and housing. Be there for meetings with bandleaders or load your iPod with the right mix of music for your party.
- **Food tester.** Sampling a caterer's menu or tasting cakes at a bakery is a fun, easy way to get involved. A fella's gotta eat, right?

Part One

THE BIG PICTURE

If you've been dating a long time, you may not be so surprised to find that your family and friends might have given more thought to your wedding than you have. Not that my mother or mother-in-law had already booked a caterer or anything, but when I did finally propose to my longtime girlfriend, Leora, everyone was incredibly relieved. Anxiously awaiting the news of our engagement, my father jokingly told the rest of my family, "If Doug doesn't ask her soon, I'll do it for him."

Leora and I did get engaged, of course, and it set in motion a year of party planning, budgeting, and decision-making that I would imagine is not unlike the preparations for a presidential inauguration. Many people had strong opinions about what needed to be done, who was responsible, and the timeline for finishing it all.

Getting engaged can sometimes feel as if you are riding the prize-winning horse at the Kentucky Derby. Just moments ago things had been going along so calmly, you've been trotting along, making your way to the starting gate. Suddenly, perhaps within moments of slipping an engagement ring on your fiancée's finger, the gate opens and you're off to the races. Only instead of merely racing toward the finish line, you can sometimes feel as if you are being chased by hundreds of wedding vendors, family members, and friends, all with specific ideas of what they think your wedding should look like.

You'll probably be faced with an incredible amount of details, most of which you have not thought about before. It's okay if you feel a tad overwhelmed. Hopefully you also feel excited and energized about getting married and are ready to enjoy being engaged. Even a short engagement lasts longer than a wedding day, so enjoy the time you spend together as an engaged couple. This is supposed to be fun.

Why Doing Nothing
Is as Important
as Anything . . . for Now

It may seem counterintuitive, but the best thing you can do right now is nothing. I know what you're thinking: "Aren't there a million things to do?" Yes, and that's precisely the reason why you, your fiancée, and your families should agree to do absolutely nothing, at least for now.

When Leora and I got engaged, we, along with our families and friends, were riding high on a wave of excitement. Recognizing that we would quickly become mired in the minutiae of event planning, I declared a one-week moratorium on wedding details. For seven days we would make no definitive plans and would hold no meetings with facility managers, bandleaders, or stationers. We would simply sit back and enjoy ourselves for at least a little while and not let a narrow focus on details take the place of our joy at getting engaged.

Your wedding moratorium need not last a week. It could be a day, a month, or any time in between. Your personality, your bride's patience, family pressure, and your specific circumstances will dictate your timeline. If you're planning a long engagement, will your plans really change if you start making them seventy-four weeks before your wedding rather than seventy-five? With all the details that are likely to dominate your conversations, taking a deep breath before you and your fiancée dive in is a great way to get started on the right foot. (But then again, if it's February and you're hoping for a spring wedding, I wouldn't recommend waiting too long lest you find that every church, temple, and even the event room at your local Motel 6 is booked solid for the next six months.)

As for my own wedding-planning moratorium, it was a good idea at least in theory. Although I had called for a time-out of one week, too many people were too excited and had too many questions for us to hold out for the entire seven days. The moratorium turned out to be no more than the proverbial finger in the dike, stemming a flood of planning and details that couldn't be ignored.

ENGAGED GROOM TIP

Wedding-Free Zones

Getting ready for your wedding can sometimes feel as if you are listening to a radio station called KWED, "All Wedding Planning, All the Time." Sometimes you'll just want to change the dial, if not throw the radio out the window altogether. Know your limitations. If you work late on Wednesdays, have a regular poker night with your friends on Fridays, or tend to fall asleep early on Sundays, perhaps one of those times would be good to choose as what I call a wedding-free zone.

What does it mean to be "wedding-free"? Exactly what it sounds like. During a time of your mutual choosing, you and your bride should talk about anything—the weather, sports, the geopolitical situation in the Korean peninsula and its effect on Asian futures trading—except your wedding. Don't talk about song lists, don't try to pick out a font for your invitation, and, for the love of everything good in this world, don't look at any color swatches. (The operative phrase in this paragraph is, of course, "a time of your mutual choosing." Remember that your fiancée might also have events she might not want to miss or nights on which she needs to just veg out in front of the TV.)

A weekly date night might be the best use of your wedding-free zone. Taking some time to check in with each other and have fun can keep you focused on why you got engaged in the first place. But just as you'd never bring work from the office on a first date, your weekly date nights should be the exclusive territory of you and your fiancée. The date night is not a time to discuss wedding plans or take cell phone calls from pushy parents. Like a carefully monitored IV drip dispensing 250 cc of perspective and relief, regularly going out for dinner, a movie, or a stroll through a park can keep both of you calm and levelheaded as your hurtle toward the big day.

Paying for the Wedding

 At this point, the only thing that you've probably paid for is the bride's engagement ring, and you most likely laid down the cash for that one months ago. Soon enough you'll be swimming across a moat of quotes, deposits, and receipts, and perhaps no other piece of information will be as important to you, your bride, and your families as the budget. In a recent survey, 43 percent of couples reported having spent more money on the wedding than they had planned, but I would argue that most of them didn't probably know exactly how much they wanted to spend in the first place. Knowing your budget before you get started will affect every decision you make and is the only way to prevent expenses—and emotions—from spiraling out of control.

The average cost of a wedding is quickly approaching $30,000 and, with the rapidly expanding wedding industry, may be even more expensive by the time you finish reading this sentence. But if you remember nothing else about that figure, remember this: *it is an average.* Six-figure weddings are not uncommon in our supersized society, but neither are more modest affairs.

Thousands of variables can affect the ultimate price of your wedding. For example, in the New York City area, you can add over $3,000 to the cost of the average wedding, while in the southeastern United States the average price is still less than $20,000 as of this writing. You can't necessarily control where you live, but there is something you can control: your own decisions. After all, which couple is smarter? The bride and groom who spend $50,000 on the wedding of the century but are still paying off credit card bills ten years later, or the couple who spend $10,000 or less and have enough left over for a down payment on a house in which to start a family?

WHO PAYS FOR WHAT?
A TRADITIONAL LOOK

Traditionally, a bride's family pays for the majority of wedding expenses, serving as hosts for the day's events. But tradition is not necessarily keeping pace with progress, and an increasing number of today's brides and grooms are paying for a part of or even their entire wedding themselves. Nevertheless, tradition is a good place from which to start, so here is a list of common wedding expenses and who typically pays for them:

Bride's Family

- Ceremony expenses: facility rental fees, flowers and decorations, music, etc.
- Reception expenses: facility rental fees, catering, bartenders, wedding cake, music, flowers and decorations, and rental items such as chairs, linens, etc.
- Bride's wedding dress
- Bridesmaids' and flower girls' bouquets
- Invitations and save-the-date announcements, including printing, addressing, and postage
- Thank-you notes, ceremony programs, seating cards, and other miscellaneous printing needs
- Photographers and videographers
- Wedding favors

Groom's Family

- Rehearsal dinner: food, music, decorations, etc.

Bride

- Groom's wedding ring
- Bridesmaids'/attendants' gifts

Groom

- Bride's wedding ring
- Groomsmen's gifts

- Tuxedo, suit, or other attire
- Mother and mother-in-law's corsages and groomsmen's boutonnieres
- Clergy/officiant's fee
- Marriage license

Despite this list, modern families make defining the word *traditional* a difficult if not impossible task. While a mother and father marrying off their only daughter might be ready to pay for 90 percent of the wedding, the parents of seven daughters might be a little less willing to open up their checkbook. The wedding you're having if you are twenty-four years old might be different from the wedding you are having if you are thirty-four. Adult children of divorced or widowed parents have still other considerations that affect the ultimate division of wedding expenses.

Today, the biggest variable that will affect your budget is likely to be you and your bride. In fact, in a recent study, almost one-third of couples paid for their weddings themselves. Fifteen percent made contributions with both sets of parents. Why is this happening? For starters, as couples get married later in life, they tend to be more settled in their careers and perhaps have a little more income at their disposals with which to cover wedding expenses. Additionally, as weddings become less a display of a woman's lifelong fantasies and more a reflection of a couple's relationship, grooms are starting to open up their wallets and put some money on the table.

Money, of course, entitles the person providing it to at least a little control. You might not have the heart to tell your future in-laws that you're allergic to shellfish if they are paying for the caterer and have their hearts set on scampi. But a groom who offers to pay for the band might have more influence about what kind of music it plays. As you are making your budget, be clear about each expense and who will pay for it. Just remember to be sensitive, too. Paying for the band doesn't mean you can ignore your in-laws' wishes by hiring your favorite death-metal band. Then again, if your future in-laws are headbangers and have a huge collection of black T-shirts, all bets are off.

MAKING A BUDGET

Using a simple spreadsheet program such as Excel, list each expense and its estimated cost. You should also in-

OUR WEDDING BUDGET

ITEM/ SERVICE	ESTIMATED COST	ACTUAL COST	PROVIDER
Reception Facility Fee	$3,000.00	$3,500.00	Lac La Belle Country Club
Flowers	$1,000.00	$1,246.90	Aviva Florists
Band	$4,000.00	$3,500.00	S. Rosenberg
Caterer	$6,000.00	$5,320.00	Barb Adams Catering
—Catering Staff Tips	$1,200.00	$1,200.00	
Wedding Cake	$650.00	$785.73	Simma's Bakery

clude fields to note any deposits paid, additional costs that are still outstanding, and due dates for making final payments. No one expects you to be a complete expert on every facet of budgeting, so don't be too concerned if you overestimate the cost of a caterer or lowball the amount you'll need for flowers. As you begin to get quotes from different vendors, you can always move money that has been freed up in one category to another. At this stage of the game, just listing your projected expenses will help you create a spending cap before you start writing any checks.

Here's a good way to format your budget:

DEPOSIT	REMAINING COST	DATE DUE	NOTES
$2,500.00	$1,000.00	1-Mar	Check or money order only
$900.00	$346.90	15-Aug	
$2,000.00	$1,500.00	29-Aug	
$2,500.00	$2,820.00	21-Aug	Includes table rentals
$0.00	$1,200.00	29-Aug	Bring cash for tips
$250.00	$535.73	15-Aug	

ITEM/ SERVICE	ESTIMATED COST	ACTUAL COST	PROVIDER
Invitations	$500.00	$471.61	Nodrog & Co. Stationers
Clergy Fee	$400.00	$400.00	Rabbi Peter Rigler
Totals:	$16,750.00	$16,424.24	

Notice that I've formatted this spreadsheet to include more than just a simple list of expenses and providers. Keeping a side-by-side comparison of your projected and actual expenses is a good way to make sure you stay within your budget. I also suggest that you keep track of payment due dates so you can prepare for a day on which you have to pay five different vendors at once without having to max out your credit cards. You might include additional columns that list the specific date when deposits were paid and, if you are splitting expenses among different family members, who will take responsibility for what.

Where should your budget begin? Traditionally the single largest expense of any wedding is the reception. Rental fees, along with the basic elements of a good party—catering, bartending, and renting chairs, tables, and linens—often account for nearly half of the average wedding budget. But if you're having a small backyard reception or can think of a less traditional place for a party, you might be able to free up a lot of money for other large expenses. (Or you might just leave that money in your bank account.)

A common mistake that many brides and grooms make

DEPOSIT	REMAINING COST	DATE DUE	NOTES
$0.00	$471.61	15-May	Must be paid in full
$0.00	$400.00	29-Aug	
$8,150.00	$8,274.24		

when building a budget is to focus solely on major expenses such as a caterer's fee or the cost of renting a function hall. Smaller expenses, such as postage for thank-you notes or the cost of copying wedding programs, might not seem like a lot when each is considered individually, but can easily equal hundreds or even thousands of dollars when taken as a whole. Set aside money for incidentals and budget a little extra to serve as a cushion against any unforeseen expenditures. It may seem Orwellian, but don't get caught off guard by "known unknowns" of wedding planning.

Don't forget a large and often overlooked part of any budget: gratuities. "We came out over budget, and it was really because of one thing," says Michael, an educator from Atlanta, Georgia. "We didn't budget enough for gratuities." I can't tell you how many brides and grooms forget this expense, which primarily goes to waiters, bartenders, and other members of your caterer's staff. Delivery people, facilities managers, valets, coat-check attendants, janitors, and other employees of the space in which you are having your wedding are usually given tips as well. You should even tip people such as bandleaders or anyone else whose services go above and beyond the call of duty. In fact, it is not unheard of for couples to make an extra donation to a church or temple if their priest or rabbi winds up being exceptionally personal and sensitive.

Even a small tip of 10 percent can be a lot when you're talking about bills that in many cases will total a few thousand dollars or more, so ask around if you aren't sure how much to give. Any professional will be honest about the normal and customary tips for his staff, and you can always ask a service provider's references for a ballpark figure. Just remember to ask for this information in advance. Michael's experience of waiting until the last minute to figure out gratuities serves as a cautionary tale. "In retrospect, I think we were overcharged, but I didn't feel like making a stink about it. How can you argue over a gratuity after you've given it?"

But let's get back to the rest of your budget. Many books and Web sites will provide you with a list of expenses down to every last swizzle stick for your cocktail hour. I am loath to give you such a list and feel that any comprehensive cataloging of wedding expenses makes people choose more, not less, causing their budgets to go up exponentially. A book that tells you to budget for valet parking may not be aware that the church at which you are getting married has a gigantic parking lot. In fact, depending on your circumstances, you and your bride may not need much more than a marriage license, someone to preside over your wedding, and a few witnesses.

Take any and all comprehensive lists not just with a grain of salt, but perhaps with an entire saltshaker. Remember that people who sell their wedding- and event-related services also create many sample budgets and expense lists and may have a vested interest in padding the lists as much as possible. As a general rule, here's a good warning for you, whether you are a wholly equal participant in the planning or a sideline player: *be wary of anyone who tells you exactly how much you* need *to spend on your wedding.*

People *need* to breathe oxygen, drink water, eat food, and get a little sunlight now and then. No one *needs* a $10,000 wedding dress or fifteen-piece orchestra. Ever since the days of Freud, psychologists have been unable to find any correlation between how much fun people have at weddings and the number of personalized napkins a couple has printed. If you want personalized napkins, fine, but don't let anyone convince you that personalized napkins are something you *need*. Wedding consultants and event planners *need* you to spend a lot of money for their businesses to grow, but the only thing you *need* is to have the wedding that you, your bride, and your families *want*.

3

Picking a Date and Venue

You can't get married unless you decide when and where you want to do
it, and an engagement that ambles
on for years without any end in sight
can begin to feel a tad tedious.
Whether you're getting married at a church, a country club,
or at city hall, the time is now for picking the date and location of your wedding. With your budget in one hand and a
calendar in the other, these decisions are arguably the most
time-sensitive and pressure-laden you will make in the entire
wedding planning. Why? Let's do some math.

FACTORING IN THE VARIABLES—
WHY YOU NEED TO PICK A DATE NOW

Let's say that n equals the number of couples married in the
United States each year. There are fifty-two weeks in a year,
but that number must be subtracted by y, where y is equal to

the number of holiday weekends such as Thanksgiving, Christmas, and, if you are a real stickler for avoiding big events, Super Bowl Sunday. (If you are Jewish and must avoid wedding-free holidays such as Rosh Hashanah and Yom Kippur, this number can be expressed as y^2.) There is also another variable, the "w factor," something that wedding experts define as directly proportional to the level of insistency on the part of your bride, grandmother, or other relative that you get married on a Saturday evening in May. The formula can be expressed as follows:

$$\frac{n}{52 - y} \ (w) = Z$$

Z, of course, equals the mathematical expression of the chances you'll have in getting the weekend you want in the Mayflower Room at the local Holiday Inn.

All kidding aside, the math is quite simple. Each year, approximately 2.2 million couples tie the knot in the United States. That's an average of over forty-two thousand each weekend, which means that if you want your choice of dates and venues, you better get cracking.

Wouldn't it be nice if picking a date were as simple as hanging a calendar on a wall and playing a game of pin-the-wedding-on-the-weekend? Unfortunately, it's never that easy. Maybe your other engaged-to-be-married friends have already snatched up a number of choice weekends for their weddings. Perhaps your fiancée's hometown pastor might be booked solid for three straight weeks. You might have to scratch off entire months depending on where you live, as summer heat or winter snow can make wearing a tuxedo uncomfortable or travel impossible.

While you and your fiancée will make many decisions without much outside influence, picking a date should not be one of them. Put out a call to immediate family, close friends, and other key players before you commit yourself to a date. You'll know which friends and family members are important enough to hold some sort of sway over when you get married and what type of events qualify as major conflicts. Your younger brother's law school graduation or your sister's due date to deliver her baby are probably good reasons to be considerate of other people's schedules, but your buddy's weekly poker game is not.

ENGAGED GROOM TIP

Three-Day Weekends and Holiday Weddings

I know what you're thinking. After going through the calendar and trying to narrow down a date, holidays like Presidents' Day, Memorial Day, July 4, and Labor Day start to look very attractive. And why wouldn't they? Three-day weekends mean vacations for everyone, which means that no one will have to miss a day of work traveling to and from your wedding. But before you circle the first weekend in September or the last weekend in May, take heed! Plenty of people are more than happy to miss work. But do you know what they aren't happy to miss? Vacations.

"I missed my family's annual Presidents' Day weekend ski trip for the first time in twelve years because I had to go to a friend's wedding," says Jonathan, a writer from Oakland, California. "My friend and I are close, so I had to go, but my mom, dad, and brothers were disappointed."

Even if no one has other plans over the holiday weekend on which you want to have your wedding, trying to find a cheap airline fare or available hotel room over Memorial Day weekend or July 4 can be difficult. It might simply be cheaper for you and your guests to avoid holidays altogether.

You can, of course, have your wedding whenever you want. No matter what date you pick, someone, somewhere, will find it inconvenient. There are only so many days in the year, and trying to accommodate every person's vacation or work schedule can be as difficult as building a sand castle during a hurricane.

LOCATION, LOCATION, LOCATION— PICKING A VENUE

If you're having an intimate affair in your in-laws' backyard, consider yourself lucky. With no deposit to put down and no facility rental fee, you've just freed up a lot of money to spend on other elements of the reception. But for most couples, renting the reception space is the single largest expense in their wedding budget.

Before you start looking at venues, you should have a general idea of how many people you expect to invite and what kind of reception you envision. Do you picture a sit-down dinner with tables set up around a large dance floor, or an extended cocktail party with a DJ spinning tunes? Don't worry about nailing down an exact guest list just yet, but you will want to throw out some round numbers before you put down a nonrefundable deposit and lock yourself into a space. A banquet hall built to fit five hundred people can easily be adapted if you plan to host only one hundred, but it doesn't work the other way around. No amount of creativity can make a room with a one-hundred-person capacity fit five hundred.

There are some important questions to keep in mind when talking to facilities managers. Many venues require that you end the party by the Cinderella-like hour of midnight, which might sound late to your grandmother Miriam and great-uncle Sidney, but can seem awfully short if your ceremony runs long and the party doesn't start until after nine o'clock. Be sure to ask how late you can keep your party going and if there are any penalties for extending it beyond the cutoff.

Ask if the facility has any "our room, our caterer" rules or a list of preferred vendors, which can either make things incredibly convenient—a sort of one-stop shopping for your major wedding needs—or complicate things immensely if you have a special menu or price limit in mind. A banquet room that has a low facilities rental fee might cover its costs by increasing its in-house caterer's per-person price. Find out if you are free to hire your own vendors, and what, if any, restrictions the room has on outside service providers.

As an Engaged Groom, picking a venue is a perfect time for you to think outside the box. So what if every couple in town is married at the local country club? You might find a better deal and a more unique experience in a museum, many of which have large gallery spaces that can easily be converted for after-hours special events. Old historic homes, universities, loft buildings, zoos, and botanic gardens often have great spaces that can provide a beautiful backdrop for your nuptials. New York's Central Park is a great place for a wedding, and reserving some green space starts at only $400 as of this writing. (Visit http://www.centralparknyc .org/thingstodo/weddings for more information.) Even small towns have more to offer than just hotels and banquet halls, so check with your local chamber of commerce for more ideas.

ENGAGED GROOM TIP

Off-Peak Weddings, Off-Peak Prices

Not only do the majority of weddings take place during the warmer months of spring, summer, and early fall, but they also overwhelmingly take place on weekends. But who says your wedding has to be on a Saturday or Sunday? In a textbook example of supply and demand, caterers, photographers, bands, and other wedding vendors often charge lower fees when their services are less likely to be needed. Have your wedding on a weeknight, and a swanky penthouse restaurant or exclusive country club's function room might be yours at a bargain-basement price. (Note that this option might only be feasible if most—if not all—of your guests live locally. Not only might your out-of-town friends and family be unable to attend a weeknight event, but they might grumble at having to make a choice between your wedding and keeping their jobs.)

YOU MAY NOW HUG THE TREES— OUTDOOR WEDDINGS

Scrapping altogether the idea of an indoor wedding and opting instead for a ceremony on the beach with a sweeping view of the ocean or on a mountaintop with panoramic vistas of valleys that stretch for miles is always a romantic idea. If nothing else, maybe there's a particularly scenic golf course in your neighborhood. Outdoor weddings can indeed be quite beautiful, but be warned. You might end up answering "I do" only when someone asks you "Do you need an umbrella?" If you and your bride are planning to become two with nature, make sure your location offers a last-minute Plan B with indoor space to shield your guests from thunderstorms, intense heat, wind, or an invasion of locusts.

ENGAGED GROOM TIP

The Pros and Cons of Destination Weddings

With family members spread out across the country and hometown ties looser than a rapper's pants, many modern couples opt for what is known as a destination wedding, which the wedding industry defines as a wedding that takes place at a location other than the bride and groom's hometown.

The advantages of a destination wedding are obvious: your event is held in a beautiful location and is likely all-inclusive. Not factoring in travel, destination weddings can be cheaper than more locally based celebrations. Your guests are also treated to a unique experience, as there is typically more for them to do at a Tuscan villa than at a hotel in Tuscaloosa.

I have a kind of Scrooge-like feeling about destination weddings, as they do not likely have much significance to a bride and groom and potentially present a huge logistical and financial challenge for guests.

Many couples fall in love with the idea of having their wedding in an exotic locale simply because they think it will be fun. That may be right, but you should be aware that having your wedding in a place where you have only the most tenuous of connections might affect who comes. The same person who will gladly fly to an out-of-the-way town in Nebraska if that's where your bride grew up might grumble about flying to even the most Edenic tropical island.

Some of your guests might not be able to afford the cost of a transatlantic flight no matter how much they want to go to your wedding. To top it off, your elderly grandmother, who has a hard enough time sleeping through the night without getting up to go to the bathroom ten times, might find it physically impossible to sit through an eight-hour flight. Is it any wonder, then, why destination weddings are typically smaller affairs than their mainland U.S. counterparts? (Of course, that fact in and of itself might be part of the allure of destination weddings.)

As with any decision you will make as an Engaged Groom, take into consideration the type of wedding you want to have and the number of people you hope will join you at your celebration. While you and your bride should ultimately do what you want, making sure you can experience your wedding with the people who are important to you will be the biggest factor in determining whether you have a destination wedding.

4

The Guest List

A guest list of two to three hundred people may seem like an unnecessary extravagance. Considering the expense and effort in organizing such an event, who would ever want such a large affair? Who can honestly say that they know enough people well enough to warrant such an enormous gathering? While John F. Kennedy may have married Jacqueline Bouvier in front of seven hundred people, most of us aren't the scions of wealthy political dynasties.

But when I got engaged, my first stab at a guest list made me nervous. My close childhood and college friends alone accounted for over thirty people, and that number almost doubled when I accounted for those who were married or in long-term relationships. Each conversation with my fiancée and our parents on the subject of the guest list yielded still more people who warranted an invite. Should my dad invite his business associates, many of whom had known me since I was in diapers? Leora's mom remembered some second cousins she hadn't seen in ten years but who might see the wedding as a good chance to reconnect with the family. What about them? Without some sort of cap, we were concerned that the guest list—and budget—would quickly spin out of control.

We decided to limit our list to 210 people, a large amount, but we expected an attrition rate of 30 to 50 people due to prior commitments or our overestimation of just how close some of these people were to us. We were aware, however, that inviting over two hundred people meant being prepared for all of them to say they could come, as sometimes even the person you thought would never attend your wedding—the second cousin once removed who lives in Alaska and rarely ventures outside his house—thinks it's worth the trip.

The 210 slots on the guest list were divided up in thirds; Leora and I were given 70, Leora's parents were given 70, and my parents were given 70. We were each free to invite whomever we wanted, as long as we didn't go over our allotted total. It meant less negotiation—"Well, if you guys are going to invite your auto mechanic, Mom's going to invite hers"—and kept the guest list under control.

Even though our system seemed to work, things are by no means one-size-fits-all. In more traditional families where the bride's family is picking up the tab, your future in-laws might demand, and rightfully deserve, a bigger slice of the guest list pie. If your parents are divorced or if your fiancée has a large number of stepsiblings, that pie might have to be cut into still more pieces.

Like most of your decisions, this one will quickly boil

down to money. A recent survey found that the average number of guests per wedding is 168. Even if you are only—only!—spending $18,000 on your wedding, that works out to be about $107 per person.

Limiting the guest lists and expenses can be tricky, but Engaged Grooms are nothing if not resourceful. "If a person didn't know both of us, we wouldn't invite them," reasoned Alan, a doctor from Milwaukee. Having been together with his fiancée, Michelle, for six years before they got engaged, Alan believed that he probably wasn't exceptionally close with anyone who hadn't met her yet. I call this the Law of Last Acquaintance: If you were close with someone in college but haven't seen him or kept in touch outside of the occasional reunion or homecoming football game, does he really warrant an invite? Other people might not make the cut, saving you even more money. Some couples don't invite children outside of their immediate family. Others rule out coworkers, lest inviting one person from the office means having to invite the whole building.

As you start making your guest list, you'll want to keep a master list. Whether you keep it or it is kept with your in-laws, make sure that it is updated as people are added to—or removed from—the guest list. You can easily format a guest list on Excel or a similar computer program, and as you get deeper into your wedding planning, you can use this list not only for addresses and invitations, but also for tracking gifts and thank-you notes and attendance at ancillary events such as a rehearsal dinner and post-wedding-day brunch.

OUR GUEST LIST

LAST NAME	FIRST NAME	STREET ADDRESS
Anderson	Nicholas and Marita	91 Eagle Pond Road
Bennett	Leigh and Scott	625 College Avenue
Birnbaum	Amy and Adam	1089 Peachtree Road
Boxt	Jason and Rosalie	456 Monument Avenue
Cunningham	Lew, Moira, Zach, and Zoe	20 Hannah Lane
Gordon	Kenneth, Dara, Michael, and Laura	10 Maple Hill Terrace
Gordon	Miriam	28 Royal Crest Street #5
Hirschfield	Irene and James	507 Park Avenue
Hirschfield	Jordan and Jody	348 Elm Street
Lerner	Sidney and Blossom	621 Summer Terrace Lane
Mates-Muchin	JT and Jacqueline	7031 Oceanview Drive
Perry	James	890 Commonwealth Avenue #1L
Rigler	Peter and Stacey	305 East 24th Street #3R
Silverman	Alan and Michelle	26 Prospect Place

CITY	STATE	ZIP CODE
New London	NH	03255
Dallas	TX	75201
Atlanta	GA	30301
Washington	DC	20008
Newton	MA	02141
Larchmont	NY	10539
Andover	MA	01812
St. Louis	MO	63101
St. Louis	MO	63102
Glen Rock	NJ	07458
Oakland	CA	94601
Boston	MA	02144
New York	NY	10036
Milwaukee	WI	53209

"AND GUEST" AND "PLUS ONE"— WHO ARE THESE PEOPLE?

Although you may have to limit your list, some people should be invited with guests no matter what. You may not like—or even know—your college buddy's new wife, but guess what? She gets invited. Here's a list of others who should get to bring a guest:

- **Married and engaged friends.** Wives, husbands, fiancées, and fiancés are always invited. In fact, as an important part of a friend's life, they shouldn't even be considered guests. When you mail the invitations, include both people's names on the envelope.
- **Domestic partners.** Friends who live with a person who in most cases would be considered a domestic partner should be an automatic "plus one."
- **Significant others of at least one year.** Be flexible if need be by making the cutoff a shorter amount of time, but avoid messy situations by being consistent across the board.
- **Groomsmen and bridesmaids.** As a courtesy, single members of the wedding party should be invited to bring a guest.
- **The awkward and uncomfortable.** I'm not talking about a cousin with some sort of social disorder or an uncle with a propensity for drooling.

I mean the random summer-camp friend, lone coworker, or old elementary-school classmate should be invited with a guest, as they will know no one at the wedding other than you and your bride.

MAIL TO THE CHIEF— INVITING CELEBRITY GUESTS

What kind of invited guest won't come to your wedding and won't even send a present? A famous one, of course. While it is technically possible to invite anyone to your wedding—and it may sometimes feel as if you are inviting *everyone* to yours—you can send invitations to world leaders, royalty, and even movie stars. They might not send you a pasta maker, but in many cases they will send you a personalized reply. If you can spare a couple of invitations for novelty's sake, here are two addresses to add to your list:

The President of the United States

The Honorable Abraham Lincoln and Mrs. Lincoln
The White House
Attn: Greetings Office
1600 Pennsylvania Avenue
Washington, DC 20500-0039

The White House will send greetings from the president and first lady after your wedding wishing you congratulations. Any invitation must include your name, home address, and the exact date of your ceremony. It also couldn't hurt to include a daytime phone number, just in case the greetings office needs to verify your information. (Depending on your political affiliation, you may feel uncomfortable using the word *honorable* before the president's name. If so, either hold off on sending an invitation to the White House or postpone your wedding until the person you vote for takes office.)

The Pope

His Holiness Benedict XVI
Prefettura della Casa Pontifica
00120 Vatican City
Italy

In a gesture of interfaith goodwill, the pontiff sends greetings to Catholics and non-Catholics alike. Just be sure to affix the proper postage to the invitation so it makes it to the Vatican. Forget about limos; you'll be the envy of your friends when you leave for your honeymoon in the Pope-mobile.

GIMME SHELTER—HOW TO HELP
YOUR GUESTS FIND A PLACE TO STAY

Travel is a part of most wedding celebrations, as just about every bride and groom has out-of-town guests. Thankfully, many hotels will reserve a large block of rooms for your event and will even offer your guests discounts off their per-night rates. Most require that you set aside a minimum of ten rooms to qualify for the preferred rate.

How many rooms will you need overall? Estimate your total number of out-of-town guests and divide that number in half, as aunts and uncles and other married relatives and friends will share rooms. If the number of rooms you need exceeds the hotel's limits, you may have to expand your reservations at other hotels. You'll probably want to do this anyway to provide options that reflect the varied finances of your guests. Reserve a block of rooms at a luxury hotel—which might be where you are having your reception—but also include nearby midpriced or economy accommodations for those on more limited budgets.

Be sure to ask if there is a deadline by when your guests must make their reservations and if they must mention a specific code or phrase, such as your last name, when booking a room. If you are asked to leave a deposit or credit card number with the hotel, ask if you will be charged for any unused rooms or if they are automatically released back into the hotel's reservation system. Even if you are told the latter is true, you should still check with the hotel as the deadline draws nearer so you don't get stuck with a gigantic bill.

You may be able to find more creative and less expensive options that go beyond name-brand hotels. A local bed-and-breakfast can give your friends and family a unique experience with pancakes and coffee included. If you are getting married in your hometown or in a city where you have a lot of friends and family, call in favors to see if people in the area will offer their spare rooms or pullout couches to your out-of-town guests.

ARRIVING ON A JET PLANE—AIRLINE AND OTHER TRAVEL DISCOUNTS

Airlines already offer what are typically known as "meeting and convention" fares for business travelers attending a professional conference or expo and have started extending those fares to wedding guests. After all, what is a wedding if not a big convention of friends and family?

Many airlines are happy to help you coordinate travel and will provide you with a code your guests can use when booking their seats. This may entitle your friends and family to receive anywhere from 5 to 10 percent off published fares. As with hotels, however, airline fares are subject to booking deadlines and sometimes-daily changes in price.

Additionally, some airlines partner with rental car companies and can help you offer discounted rates for those guests who may need to provide their own transportation to and from the airport and around town.

5

Food, Booze, Music, Flowers (Yes, Flowers), and Other Details

What makes a good party? Food? Check. Alcohol? Yep. Good music? Absolutely. As much as you might not want to get involved with them, even flowers can enliven the most exciting of parties. With so many elements to coordinate, putting together your wedding reception can seem like a Herculean task.

Just as you might hire a contractor when remodeling a kitchen because you don't know anything about plumbing, masonry, and electrical wiring, some couples hire wedding planners for assistance in planning their event. It is by no means necessary and in some cases will do little more than add another significant expense to your budget. With the right amount of communication, coordination, and cooperation there is no reason why you, your bride, and your families can't become the ultimate do-it-yourselfers.

But unless you've done this before—and hopefully you haven't—you can't just call up a bunch of contacts from within your electronic organizer. Many couples don't know where to begin, and finding a good band or caterer can be the most intimidating part of the whole wedding planning. Except for florists and bakeries, most wedding vendors don't usually have storefront businesses on Main Street, so ask around and do your homework.

The best place to start with is the venue in which you are holding your reception. Talk to the site's event manager. He or she should be familiar with a large variety of caterers, bands, and photographers who have worked there before. If you've been to any weddings that you really enjoyed recently, ask the bride and groom who made dinner. You can let your fingers do the walking by looking in phone directories or on the Internet for a DJ. Some cities even host annual wedding trade shows where dozens or even hundreds of wedding-related professionals—everyone from caterers to limo companies—set up booths to hawk their wares and compete for the business of eager brides and grooms.

More than anything, you should remember that you are hiring people to perform a job. Not that you want to be a taskmaster, but as the one holding the purse strings—or wallet, if you prefer—you're in charge. Of course, you should be reasonable, but anyone who doesn't cooperate with a legitimate request in a timely manner doesn't deserve your hard-earned money. There are plenty of courteous and professional caterers, bands, and other event specialists who are more than willing to provide you with exactly the services you want.

As you would when hiring any employee, ask for references before signing a contract or, more important, before putting down a deposit. Anyone who's been in the event business long enough should quickly be able to provide no less than three references. In fact, you should ask to be steered to clients who hosted events within the last three months, as even a bad caterer or bandleader could cherry-pick a few good reviews from years' worth of terrible service. Anyone who is not forthcoming about past jobs or who doesn't have a list of former clients on file is not to be trusted, especially considering the financial and emotional investment you, your bride, and your families are making in your wedding day.

You, or whoever is paying for specific expenses, will undoubtedly be required to pay a deposit to all service providers you hire for your wedding. That means the rest will be paid either immediately before your reception begins, upon the completion of your party, or within a short time after your wedding day. Talk with all vendors about payment schedules and get a receipt for any money you are required to pay in advance. Just because your contract says that a deposit of 50 percent is required before the wedding doesn't mean that you should leave it to other people to keep track of your money.

If you have any balances due on the day of the wedding, be sure that those making the final payments bring checks or extra cash to cover the bills. But even if you are paying for everything, don't take on this job yourself. You and your bride will most likely be too busy saying good-bye to friends and family at the end of your party to deal with finances. Prewrite your checks and assign a responsible family member or friend—a parent or best man, perhaps—to settle up with caterers or bands who expect to be paid before they pack up and go home. (If a bill must be paid within, say, a week following your event but you'll be on your honeymoon for two weeks, make arrangements for payment before you get on the plane to Fiji.

FOOD, GLORIOUS FOOD—THE CATERER

Watching the same meal being served to two hundred or more people at once is something most of us only experience at an elementary school cafeteria, summer camp dining hall, or military mess hall. Even at weddings or large events, the caterer who can make hundreds of plates of salmon or beef as good as the single serving you might have in a restaurant is a rare breed indeed. More than any other wedding expense, when it comes to catering, you get what you pay for.

Unlike smaller wedding details, food is the one thing at your party with which virtually every guest will have a direct experience . . . and a strong opinion. For that reason, don't rely on verbal assurances or pictures of plates of food from evasive caterers. When it comes to picking the person who will feed your guests, only your taste will tell.

Typically, a caterer will cook you a sample meal either at your home or in their business's headquarters. For many brides and grooms, this can be one of the best experiences in all the planning. Think about it: you call a caterer, tell him that you are getting married, set up an appointment, and before you know it, you and your bride—and possibly your parents—are being served a gourmet meal by a professional chef whose only goal is to win your business. In a brief meeting at a caterer's kitchen, you might get better service than you'd receive at even the most expensive five-star restaurant in town.

Of course, food is not only about taste but also about presentation. Even the most mouthwatering food won't be too appetizing if it's slopped onto plates like day-old gruel at an orphanage. When talking to caterers, don't forget to focus on questions that have to do with service and professionalism. Most chefs will have a team of waiters and prep cooks with whom he or she works regularly. How would he or she describe the staff? Are they foodies or a rotating roster of teenagers working a summer job? How will the waiters be dressed? How many people does he or she have to help with the event? You don't want an overworked and overstressed waitstaff, but neither do you want to pay for a bunch of bow-tie-clad waiters to stand around with nothing to do.

Some of the things you'll discuss with your caterer are whether you plan to have a sit-down dinner or a buffet, and whether that dinner will be preceded with passed appetizers or different food stations at which your guests will graze. Remember one important thing: a caterer who is capable of serving a gourmet, sit-down dinner will almost always be just as capable of preparing a delicious buffet, but it doesn't always work the other way around. Caterers who are only used to offering buffets might not have the experience to present an attractive plate of food and, perhaps even more likely, won't have a loyal team of experienced waiters to help bring those plates to the tables with grace and courtesy. If you like the way someone's food tastes but aren't sure how it will look at your wedding, ask if you can watch the caterer's setup for another event. Without being too intrusive, you might be able to watch from behind the scenes as a team of cooks and waiters prepare and plate dinner for a large number of people.

What should you serve? Obviously you'll want food that will appeal to as many different palates as possible, and that's why many couples stick with the tried-and-true and offer some variation of either chicken, beef, or fish. But deciding what kind of food to serve is a chance for some true creative thinking. You'll probably want what you serve to match the atmosphere of the party, so pizza and make-your-own sundaes might not be the way to go if everyone is wearing black tie. Still, you have some options beyond plated salmon. If you are having a buffet, why not offer a pasta with a choice of different sauces? Food is always a great way to highlight varied cultural and ethnic backgrounds, so if one type of cuisine has special meaning to your family, see if the caterer knows how to make your favorite dish.

In an earlier section, I mentioned gratuities. Ask your caterer if tips are built into the fee or if you are expected to bring cash to hand out at the end of your reception. If your caterer employs a headwaiter, he or she might be able to distribute this money on your behalf so no one has to track down every last waiter after the party is over. It is perfectly acceptable to ask a caterer exactly how much his staff expect to get. A good one will always be honest with you, unafraid to talk about money. Either way, you should be sure to ask all references for a ballpark figure or percentage when checking a caterer's bona fides.

HAVE YOUR CAKE . . .

To say that I have a sweet tooth would be an understatement. Of all the decisions Leora and I had to make during our wedding planning, no one was surprised that I liked picking a wedding cake the most. During a winter day in and around Milwaukee, Leora, her parents, and I drove from bakery to bakery, sampling no fewer than ten pieces of cake at three different bakeries. Our Midwest Gluttonfest left me with such an incredible sugar high that I practically needed to be checked into rehab for the confectionary-addicted when it was all over. It was like having a multicourse meal of cake for breakfast, lunch, and dinner! The free coffee the bakeries gave us to wash it all down was just icing on the cake. Or something like that.

Can you stick with your caterer and just have the person who is making dinner make dessert? Maybe, but it's more likely that you'll hire an independent bakery for the traditional wedding cake. If you aren't sure where to find a good baker, you can follow the usual route of asking friends or searching online, but don't be afraid of offending your caterer by asking for a recommendation. Your caterer may make all sorts of desserts, from chocolate-covered strawberries to petits fours and other pastries, but the right wedding cake sometimes requires the work of a different professional.

Wedding cakes aren't cheap, and just as you can't pick up an original Picasso or Monet for the price of a greeting card, don't be surprised if you experience a little sticker shock when pricing cakes. In fact, your jaw might drop at prices that can soar to over $10 or $15 a slice. Don't panic. Many cakes cost far less than that, and even if you look near and far and only find cakes that require you to take a bank loan, there are some alternatives.

Your baker may be able to create a small display cake for use in a cake-cutting ceremony, but make sheet cakes from the same ingredients for serving the rest of your guests. In fact, no rule says the cake you display is the cake you have to serve. As long as the sheet cake tastes the same as the display model, your guests will be none the wiser and you'll save a few bucks.

Another option for the frugal is to scout local culinary schools for emerging talent. Many schools have pastry divisions, filled with eager students ready to jump at the chance to prove their talents. The two hundred people coming to your wedding might be the largest number of people they've ever baked for in their nascent careers, so be sure to ask a school's administrators and instructors for information about their most responsible and professional students.

With any baker, make sure you are clear about all fees, schedules, and delivery procedures. Many bakeries can only accommodate a small number of weddings per weekend, so what is the deadline for hiring their services? What kind of deposit will you have to leave? On the day of your wedding, how will the cake be delivered and what are the delivery charges? Does the cake have to be kept at a specific temperature? Be aware that some facilities and caterers charge a "cake cutting" fee for divvying up the cake to serve to your guests. If the bakery is delivering the cake but not serving it, coordinate with your caterer to have someone available to accept the delivery and properly store or display the cake until it is ready to be served.

Traditionally, the top tier of a wedding cake is saved and frozen and eaten by you and your bride on your first anniversary. But why wait? There's always room for dessert, so get your marriage off to a sweet start by sharing a piece with your new wife upon your return from your honeymoon while your cake still has some flavor. Of course, if your wedding takes place hundreds or thousands of miles away, getting your cake home might not be easy, but there's nothing a little creative packaging, dry ice, and overnight shipping can't handle. Nevertheless, if preserving your cake will be too difficult or if you're worried about the health effects of eating defrosted, year-old buttercream, you can always surprise your wife with a miniature reproduction made for your anniversary by bringing a picture of your original cake to a local bakery.

Remember, no rule dictates what kind of cake you have to have or even that you have to have a cake at all. Some couples prefer cupcakes or Italian pastries and have bakers creatively stack the paper-wrapped confections in the shape of a real cake. Cupcakes are easier to serve—no slicing— and can be carried with much more grace than a cake slice on a plate with a fork. Cakes made from chocolate chip cookies and even doughnuts are not uncommon. Talk about your preferences with your fiancée, but don't worry if she has her heart set on a fondant-iced cake with dragées. As you'll see on the next page, there is room for compromise.

. . . AND EAT IT, TOO— WHAT'S A GROOM'S CAKE?

Perhaps you've been to a wedding where a tiered and elegantly decorated white cake was accompanied by a squat, hastily frosted glob that might resemble a cake if only it had some sort of discernible, describable shape. Unless there was an accident in the kitchen, what you most likely saw was a groom's cake.

Traditionally a gift from the bride to the groom and a staple at Southern antebellum weddings, the groom's cake was historically a single-layered, dark fruitcake that was sliced up and placed in boxes to be given to guests at the end of the reception. In a story reminiscent of the tooth fairy, it was believed that if a single woman put a slice of this cake under her pillow that night, she would have a dream in which she would see the man she was certain to marry. Of course, we now know that the only thing the single woman could be sure of if she did this was that her pillowcase would be covered with frosting by morning.

No longer a remnant of the old South, today groom's cakes are found at parties across the country. Fruitcakes, however, are about as popular now as they are at Christmas, and just like that messy pile of pastry and icing you may have seen, groom's cakes now take any shape, form, and flavor. Chocolate is a popular choice and nicely complements a formal white wedding cake, but whether you're partial to carrot cake, ice cream cake, or giant piles of chocolate chip cookies, the groom's cake should reflect your tastes. It can even reflect your interests.

What do I mean? Groom's cakes are a perfect opportunity for you and your bride to show off your lighter side. Many groom's cakes have been shaped as footballs, *Star Wars* characters, college mascots, or even the groom's home state. (Colorado is an easy one for bakers. Michigan, not so much.)

Still, some sticklers for formality see serving a robot-shaped cake at a black-tie wedding as the height of low class. If no one wants to serve a groom's cake at your formal reception, compromise by having it for dessert at the rehearsal dinner or by breaking it out at a late-night after-party when your more highfalutin guests have gone to sleep.

Your groom's cake can be ordered from the same bakery that is providing your wedding cake, but considering the odd shapes and flavors it might take, there's no reason why it can't be ordered at a local grocery store or baked by a friend to save a few bucks. No matter where the cake comes from, your bride may want to preserve one part of the tradition by ordering it herself and surprising you with the flavor, style, and theme.

BOOZE OR LOOSE—ALCOHOL, SOFT DRINKS, AND BARTENDING

Having the right amount of beverages—alcoholic or otherwise—is another key to a successful party. Any good caterer will know exactly how to stock a bar so that it is equipped to serve all of your guests for the duration of your party, but if you are taking on the responsibility yourself, there are some things you should know.

At a party, people typically consume one to two drinks per hour. This figure accounts for fraternity brothers who like to binge drink, your cousins who'd like to bring back Prohibition, and everyone in between. So, if you have a cocktail hour with two hundred guests before the main reception, you'll not only need the right mixers but also supplies—glassware, corkscrews, tongs, napkins, garnishes, and a lot of ice—to create anywhere from two hundred to four hundred drinks during that hour. At the reception, drinking might slow down a bit for a brief time as your guests become more focused on eating or dancing, but the same guest-to-drink ratio applies. If you are having a champagne toast, one case of bubbly pours about seventy-five glasses.

No one likes to wait a long time for a drink, especially if all a person plans to order is a Coke or Shirley Temple. For that reason, make sure you have the right number of bar stations and bartenders to handle the traffic flow. Your two-hundred-person reception should be covered by three to four bars, which should be spaced so as to prevent bottlenecks near the dance floor, exits, and other key locations. To keep the lines short, have waiters pass out wine or specialty drinks from trays as they walk among your guests.

Obviously, the style of wedding you plan to have will dictate your alcohol and bartending needs. A white-tie affair might require white-gloved waiters, but a backyard barbecue might require nothing more than some big tubs of ice and a few cases of microbrews.

As with any wedding service provider, be sure to ask the right questions of whoever is handling alcohol and other beverages at your party. Is there a by-the-drink fee or is the price all-inclusive? Does the fee include tips to bartenders and servers? What brands of alcohol are used to stock the bars? Is there a fee for any unopened bottles or can they be returned? Most important, and especially if you are having an outside caterer serve alcohol to your guests, does he or she have the requisite liquor license and insurance to comply with local ordinances?

In discussing alcohol with a caterer, special events manager, or other service provider, you might hear something about a "corkage fee." This is a fee, levied on people who provide their own bottles of wine or other alcohol, to open and serve such bottles. So, if your father-in-law has a connection with a wholesaler who can get a few cases of bubbly at cost, a corkage fee might wind up costing more per bottle than each bottle itself! Do the math before you decide to buy four cases of wine on your own.

A note on etiquette: *it is never acceptable to have a cash bar at a wedding.* It might save you money, but it will annoy your guests. In fact, after the time they spend getting to your wedding and the money they spend on a gift, all they might want is a stiff drink. No one expects to pay for anything at a wedding, and you don't want to send your guests searching for the nearest ATM. If you need to save money, offer a limited number of top-shelf or premium alcoholic brands, serve sparkling wine instead of genuine French champagne, choose the house wine rather than an imported vintage, or limit your alcoholic options to just wine and beer.

IF MUSIC BE THE FOOD OF LOVE—
HIRING A BAND OR DJ

From the local pub and trendy bar to a hot nightclub and swanky lounge, nothing sets the mood for a party like good tunes. But your wedding isn't just any party, and having a good time isn't necessarily as simple as tuning the radio to your favorite Top 40 station. You may want to leave the music to a professional. (Although iPods and other MP3 players are making anything possible. More on that later.)

Stuart Rosenberg, a musician and producer based in Chicago, Illinois, takes a somewhat philosophical approach when he plays a wedding . . . and he plays over fifty of them a year. "Music is the lens of joy for the human spirit. Long after the rubber chicken is forgotten, people will remember the physical expression of joy that music allows, and choosing the right musicians will allow the energy of a gathering to bloom like a brilliant flower in the sunshine." But that energy will only bloom if you remember that you are inviting everyone from your youngest cousin to your most senior grandparent. As a result, you'll need to find someone who can play the kind of music that can appeal to multiple generations and personalities. It's not always easy. The band you love listening to at your local watering hole may have absolutely no idea how to play to a roomful of geriatrics.

Of course, you might be wondering if you even need a band. Can't you have a DJ? Absolutely. In fact, hiring a DJ is usually easier on your wallet, as the typical jock only has to bring CDs or an MP3 player, stereo equipment, and speakers, whereas a ten-piece orchestra comes with a lot more logistical concerns and, obviously, higher fees. Musical purists might want to hear the original versions of their favorite songs, and the only way to get that is with a DJ. Then again, bands can often provide more entertaining performances and are typically better at motivating your guests to dance. DJs can provide hours of continuous musical entertainment, but bands have to take breaks every now and then. The list of pros and cons in the band-versus-DJ debate could go on forever, so at a certain point you'll have to make a decision. Like Smokey Bear's rule about forest fires, only you can decide what's right for your party.

But how do you even find good wedding entertainment? Stuart has this suggestion: "The best way to choose your musicians is by personal experience." That means if you went to a wedding or other special event recently and enjoyed the band, you should ask the party's organizer for a contact number. Nothing will assure you and your bride of a band's skill like having been at a party where they played before. Since picking music is probably one of the most subjective tasks of all wedding planning, the best thing to trust is your own ears.

That doesn't necessarily mean you should pick your favorite bar band or street-corner folksinger to play at your wedding. If the function of your band will be to provide music for a low-key reception, hiring the jazz combo you hear on your commute to work might be a perfectly adequate and inexpensive option. You can also contact local conservatories or graduate schools with strong music programs if all you'll need is someone to provide background music for an extended cocktail hour. But if you're hoping for music and dancing to take a more central role in your party, go with a band that has some experience playing weddings.

Don't panic if you haven't heard anything mind-blowing recently. Stuart suggests asking friends who share your musical tastes or whose tastes you trust. The key may be to cast a wide demographic net and take suggestions from friends and family. Don't just talk to your college buddies or siblings. Your parents may have heard a good band or DJ lately and will probably have strong opinions when it comes to music. After all, they might want to dance at your wedding more than you do. If all else fails, Stuart recommends asking the people who have undoubtedly been to hundreds of weddings in your area: the caterer, photographer, and other service providers you've hired. "They've heard everything and know what's out there," he says.

If you opt for a band, you'll probably want to see them live before you make a commitment and may even want to see them in their natural habitat, a wedding. If a bandleader offers to let you see them play someone else's wedding, make sure he gets permission from the other bride and groom and their families before you go. If they say yes, do your best to blend in and stay out of the way once you're there; don't show up in jeans and a T-shirt for someone else's black-tie affair. Despite what you may have heard, however, going to someone else's wedding to hear a band is not an option most good bands will even offer. "Would you want them inviting strangers to your wedding?" asks Stuart. Touché.

A band might offer you a demo recording or direct you to a Web site where you can listen to audio samples. Don't let either one be the only criterion on which you base your decision. A poor recording might cause you to rule out a perfectly good band, while a slickly produced CD can make even the worst-sounding garage band sound as if they are ready for their close-up on MTV. Be especially cautious about demo recordings if you work with an agency or an office that represents multiple bands. The band you'll get at your wedding might not be the band you heard on your headphones. "Oftentimes the office has one or two demos that they send out to all who inquire," says Stuart, "and clients are sent whatever band is next up on their list."

It's a good idea to meet with the bandleader or DJ in person before you hire him. This may be the only way for you to see if your personalities and musical philosophies jibe. "Good bandleaders will want to represent your musical sensibility, as opposed to inflicting theirs on you," says Stuart. A good way to help you in this regard is to make a giant wish list of the songs you'd like to hear. Call it your dream jukebox. A band might not be able to play every song on your list, but knowing that you and your families like Marvin Gaye and Stevie Wonder will prompt them to polish the Motown classics in their repertoire.

Knowing that weddings are highly personal affairs, most bands will be happy to learn one or more songs not already in their bag of tricks. If you and your bride have "your song" and hope to dance to it at your wedding, give the band ample time to rehearse it. You might also surprise your parents by finding out what songs were played at their weddings and having your band learn them for spotlight dances. A DJ, of course, should have no problem tracking down even the most special of special requests.

On the flip side, don't forget to tell your bandleader or DJ what songs you absolutely don't want to hear. You probably won't be shy about telling a caterer if you don't want tilapia, scrod, or other unfortunately named fish for dinner, so don't be shy about making your musical preferences known. (See the sample Do Not Play List on pages 65–67.)

When you do meet with the bandleader or DJ, go beyond the basic musical questions. How much space does the band need and how much time will it need to set up and break down? How many breaks do they take? Do they need to be fed? Can the band provide music for the ceremony or will you have to hire a string quartet? How much will it cost if you decide to keep the party going long after the hour agreed upon in your contract or does the DJ turn into a pumpkin after midnight? A band will likely have microphones for its singers, but does the DJ have some sort of PA system if you are having people make toasts? While you shouldn't get mired down too much in the technical, find out if there are any special wiring needs that might be beyond the capacity of your venue. You'd hate to have the DJ show up an hour before the party only to find that he can't plug in his speakers without blowing a fuse.

Most important, and as you would with any service provider, discuss any and all fees. If you're worried that a band's or DJ's fees seem too cheap to be true, don't ignore that feeling. Sure, you might want to save money in as many areas as possible, but with music being the backbone of any good party, you might not want to skimp on this expense. A wedding held in a junkyard with a great band might be a lot more fun than a wedding held at a fancy country club with a bad one. Stuart agrees. "Beware of musicians willing to undercut the market and offer you their services for a much lower price than the competition. This is almost certainly an indication that these are part-time musicians or 'weekend warriors.' Do you really want amateurs playing for you?" Ask how long the musicians have been playing together. Most good wedding bands have had the same lineup for years.

Of all the people at your wedding, bandleaders take a larger role than even some of your family members. Just don't let anyone hog the spotlight. The stars of your wedding should be you and your bride, not some Harry Connick Jr. wannabe. DJs usually have good personalities, but you don't probably want yours to be as chatty as Casey Kasem. If you need someone to introduce toasts or instruct guests to sit down when a course is served, let your bandleader or DJ know exactly what you want him to do and be clear about the limits of his role. Provide a written schedule of the party's events and include a list of people's names and pronunciations if he has to do introductions. As an Engaged Groom, you might have one more concern: how you and your bride are introduced when you make your grand entrance. Leora did not take my name when we got married, and we did not want our bandleader to introduce us as "Mr. and Mrs. Doug Gordon." You may decide to do away with introductions altogether, as the less time a bandleader spends emceeing, the more time there is for him to actually play music.

Ultimately, the band or DJ you choose should strike a delicate balance between keeping your guests entertained and blending seamlessly into the fabric of your reception. As Stuart so wisely points out, "The consequence of making the right choice is not having your guests leaving the party and saying, 'What a great band,' it's having your guests leaving the party and saying, 'What a great party!' "

ENGAGED GROOM TIP

iPod, Therefore iAm

Even though the best bandleaders and DJs can add an incalculable value to your party, there is one value that most can calculate, and that is their fee. For less formal gatherings where dancing and music might not be as important, there is a low-cost option: an iPod or other digital music player. Load one up with a few hours of your favorite tunes, hook it up to a good sound system, and you're ready to party. If you're concerned with satisfying all the different musical tastes of your guests, solicit requests from friends and family in the months leading up to your wedding and add the songs that you and your fiancée think everyone will most enjoy. Make play lists of romantic songs, big-band numbers, old standards, and modern rock and pop and have some of your friends man the buttons.

Whether you use it to play a few jazz standards during your cocktail hour or as the main source of music for your reception, not only will you save hundreds if not thousands of dollars, but you'll be able to grab the little gadget on your way out of the reception and listen to it as you take a long plane ride to New Zealand.

HEY, DJ, STOP PLAYING THAT SONG— THE MOST INAPPROPRIATE SONGS TO PLAY AT YOUR WEDDING

An Engaged Groom knows that just because a song has a good beat doesn't mean it's appropriate at a celebration honoring a couple's love, commitment, and new life together. In fact, the best love songs are more likely than not about heartbreak. So caveat emptor. If you're going to pick a song to be played during your first dance as husband and wife, you might want to listen to the lyrics first. With that warning in mind, you may have heard some of these songs played at other people's weddings. Don't play them at yours, and don't be shy about including them on a Do Not Play List that you give to a bandleader or DJ.

- **"I Will Always Love You," Dolly Parton.** Maybe you're more familiar with Whitney Houston's version. What you might not know is that this song is about a breakup.
- **"My Heart Will Go On," Celine Dion.** Any song that will forever be associated with a movie about a sinking ship is not the best sound track for your marriage.
- **"Wonderful Tonight," Eric Clapton.** The song seems innocent enough, so much so that it's become a cliché at a lot of weddings, but it ends

with the singer unable to drive home or to put himself to bed because he's stoned, drunk, or both.

- **"I Can't Make You Love Me," Bonnie Raitt.** But I will make you marry me.
- **"More Than Words," Extreme.** Cheesy but romantic? Maybe. Sung from the perspective of a guy pressuring his girlfriend to have sex? Really. Read the lyrics.
- **"Against All Odds," Phil Collins.** In this song, Phil is coming to terms with the fact that his girlfriend's return is highly unlikely, making this song perfect for your wedding . . . if you've been ditched at the altar.
- **"Every Breath You Take," The Police.** The favorite of people marrying their stalker.

But those are just the slow songs. Some party anthems and disco classics can be just as inappropriate, so if you must hear them at your wedding, save these songs for a late-night karaoke session at the hotel bar. A small sampling:

- **"I Will Survive," Gloria Gaynor.** The most commonly played dance song and the most inappropriate for a wedding. I'm willing to bet you don't want your new wife out on the dance floor singing, "Walk out the door / Just turn around now / 'cause you're not welcome anymore."
- **"Billie Jean," Michael Jackson.** Songs about illegitimate children are never appropriate at weddings.

- **"I Heard It Through the Grapevine," Marvin Gaye.** A staple of Motown medleys and get-down groove sessions, but just remember that the thing that Marvin heard through the grapevine is that his lady friend has been cheating on him.
- **"Who Are You," The Who.** To be played at arranged marriages only.
- **"You Oughta Know," Alanis Morissette.** A call to arms for any woman who's ever been jilted by a guy, and one to avoid for any newly married couple. It's especially dangerous to play this one if you are inviting an ex-girlfriend to the wedding.
- **"50 Ways to Leave Your Lover," Paul Simon.** Make a new plan, Stan, and leave this one off your list.
- **"Why Don't We Get Drunk (and Screw)," Jimmy Buffett.** No comment.

WHERE HAVE ALL THE FLOWERS GONE?—THE FLORIST

Although as an Engaged Groom you may be somewhat progressive in nature, progress has not exactly caught up to you when it comes to an encyclopedic knowledge of flora. Chances are you can't tell the difference between a peony and a petunia, but even if you do have opinions on color, size, or style, chances are even better that your bride will make most of the arrangements—pun intended—with the florist herself.

Even a man steeped in the botanical sciences may find it

hard to communicate his ideas to a section of the wedding industry still regarded as exclusively feminine. When Leora and I sat down to meet with our florist months before our wedding, the shop's wedding coordinator spoke only to my fiancée, hardly acknowledging me beyond our initial introduction and exchange of pleasantries. When I had a question, the woman directed her answers to Leora, as if my fiancée were some sort of UN interpreter, and the only person with access to a florist-to-English dictionary.

If you are worried about finding yourself in a similar position, do your homework. Get a feel for different types of flowers and their names by looking at online flower services such as 1800Flowers.com. If you are attending any other weddings in the coming months, take a minute to notice the flowers. At the ceremony, what do the boutonnieres look like? At the reception, how big are the centerpieces? Can you see the person sitting across the table from you or does a giant bouquet block your view? Although you may not be able to articulate every last feeling you have about the flowers, you should at least be able to trust your intuition about what looks good and what does not.

Ask questions as you would of any vendor. Do you have to make up your mind on every last vase and arrangement now or can you change your order later if need be? Who will deliver the flowers, and what time will he or she need to access the space in which you are getting married and holding your reception? Will the florist take care of decorating the room or will he or she have to coordinate delivery and setup with a building facility manager? Some florists consider vases items for purchase while others rent them for a smaller fee. Will you be required to purchase the vases in which the centerpieces are held or does the florist expect them to be returned after the party? Be sure to check all references and discuss all fees and payment schedules before signing a contract.

SAY CHEESE—PICKING A PHOTOGRAPHER

From early-morning preparations to the ceremony and reception, perhaps no other wedding service provider will have as much direct interaction with you, your bride, your families, and your guests throughout your wedding day as the photographer. Depending on how much effort you make to be social, some of your guests will have more interaction with your photographer than they will with you and your bride.

Don't think that all wedding photographers are created equal. In fact, don't think you can get away with calling someone a wedding photographer just because he takes photographs at weddings. Depending on his style, he may prefer the term *wedding photojournalist.*

Scott Patrick, one such professional based in Milwaukee, has his own particular take on finding a person who jibes with your style and budget. "Couples should ask a lot of questions," advises Scott, but the important thing is to ask the right ones.

"Brides tend to like answers to the more emotional questions of style and approach, whereas grooms tend to like answers to the more technical questions like 'How long will you be with us?' 'How many pictures will you take?' and, of course, 'How much money will it cost?' " Neither approach, Scott cautions, is wholly correct. Every question a couple asks "needs to be packaged with the other less tangible qualities, because if you simply select the cheapest photographer, you will get the cheapest quality and service. Will any amount spent be worth it if you are unhappy with the results?"

Scott cautions people from delving too far into the technical components of a photographer's services. In most cases, this information is of little use to even the biggest techno-geeks. "The question that is nearly pointless but that so many magazines and Web sites think a couple should ask is 'What type of equipment do you use?' To me, that is like asking a mechanic what brand of wrench he uses." Instead of getting hung up on whether a photographer has the latest gadgetry, "look at the work and get a feeling for who the photographer is as an artist and person." Beyond asking whether the photographer shoots on film, with a digital camera, or with a combination of both, knowing the precise technical specs of his cameras will do little to assure a couple that a photographer can take good pictures. "The camera is merely a tool," says Scott, "and if a photographer has to monkey with his gear all of the time, then he will miss what is going on."

A wedding is a great time to make a pictorial history of your family, and many brides and grooms take great pains to set aside time before or after the ceremony to pose with groups of grandparents, siblings, or distant relatives. Making a list of all the pictures you and your families want will help your photographer immensely and prevents you from later receiving an album and wondering why there isn't a picture of your great-grandmother. To ensure that you get everyone you want into every picture, it's a good idea to recruit a couple of family members or friends to corral people for specific groupings. Even with a detailed list, your photographer will not be able to tell your cousins from your college buddies, so having a family member pick up this job is one way to guarantee that no one is left out.

Still, Scott advises brides and grooms not to spend too much time taking formal portraits. "When you dream of your wedding, do you dream about striking a pose hundreds of times in different locations and smiling into the camera all day?" Capturing the more spontaneous moments of a wedding is any good photographer's MO, and it's those moments that will really surprise you when you see the final pictures.

Talk with your photographer about what kind of role you want him to play at the wedding. A good one will blend into the scenery, but you should still be clear about how present you want him to be at certain moments. When your bride walks down the aisle in all her glory, you don't want your view of her blocked by a shutter-happy photographer.

Don't forget that your photographer arguably has the most physically demanding job of any of your many service providers. Wedding singers take breaks, florists drop off your flowers and leave, and even waiters often have time to grab a quick snack between courses. Not so wedding photographers. If you've ever seen a wedding photographer in action, it may seem as if he is everywhere at once. That's because he has to be. Can you imagine the disappointed—and potentially bloodthirsty—parents he'd have to face if he missed the bride and groom's first dance?

Because of the physical demands of his job and the fact that he'll be photographing everything from the moment your bride puts on her makeup to the minute you ride off into the sunset at the end of the day, find out if your photographer's contract stipulates that he be provided with a meal during the reception.

As far as what happens after the wedding, discuss fees for albums and reprints ahead of time. As a professional photographer, the person you hire may technically own all the copyrights to your pictures, making it expensive for you to order reprint after reprint. Considering the number of photographers who now shoot almost exclusively with digital cameras, find out if previews of your pictures will only be available online. For those of us who have more or less grown up on the Internet, poring over pictures online before ordering reprints or putting together an album might be fine, but your parents or in-laws may want to get their hands on actual proofs.

ENGAGED GROOM TIP

Disposable Cameras

Having disposable cameras spread around the tables during your reception is a practice I like to file under "Seemed Like a Good Idea at the Time." I bet whoever came up with the idea first sure thought he was clever and takes a private delight every time he attends a wedding or event and sees a bunch of giddy guests enjoying themselves with disposable cameras. "I thought of that," the person says to himself with great pride as everyone clicks away.

There's no question that your guests will have a good time with disposable cameras, but the reality is that such pictures rarely come out the way you'd hoped. Even if you do get some keepers, the few that make the cut won't necessarily be worth the money you'll have to spend developing every roll. Leora and I had disposable cameras at our wedding, and a few got into the hands of our four-year-old niece. We wound up with seventy-two pictures of people's legs and the undersides of tables.

That's not to say you should dispense with the idea of disposable cameras altogether, but if you're looking to save money, this is a good place to do it. Forty or so cameras spread over twenty tables can quickly add up to a lot of developing fees. At some parties, guests think the disposable cameras are wedding favors and take them home. If that happens, good luck ever seeing those pictures again.

The people who are most capable of taking good pictures will probably bring their cameras anyway, and while you want your guests to relax and have fun, don't be shy about asking them to snap a few candids. With digital cameras so commonplace, your friends will probably take a lot of pictures and post them online when they get home. Using your favorite photo-sharing Web site, you can take your pick from their candid shots and save money by printing only the pictures you want. You'll also be able to selectively edit pictures by discreetly deleting any embarrassing shots before they are e-mailed to your in-laws.

Some traditions, even new ones, die hard, and someone might insist that you have disposable cameras available for your guests to use at your reception. Don't put your foot down too hard on this one. If you're worried about the expense, take heart in the fact that the developing and processing fees might be taken care of while you're on your honeymoon.

WE OUGHTA BE IN PICTURES— VIDEOGRAPHERS AND WEDDING VIDEOS

When choosing a videographer to shoot your wedding, you'll ask many of the same questions you ask of a photographer. Concentrate on the videographer's style and personality. How present is he or she at the wedding? Will you step out onto the dance floor for your first dance and be blinded by a spotlight? Will you run down the steps of the church and smack into a camera lens? Most important, ask to see samples of his or her work; it's the only way to see if the promises a videographer makes in person or on the phone match up with what he or she can actually deliver.

To pick someone to videotape our wedding, Leora and I spent one night watching a compilation of sample videos shot by various professional videographers. Despite the zeal with which I dove into other aspects of the wedding planning, I did not have a great deal of enthusiasm for this. To be honest, I'm not sure how often I'll watch my own wedding video, and if there's anything more boring than watching wedding videos of people you know, it's watching wedding videos of people you don't know. Nevertheless, one Saturday night when most couples were at the actual movies, Leora and I sat in our living room watching anonymous wedding movies. One couple fed each other wedding cake to the sounds of Celine Dion's "Because You Loved Me." Another bride and groom danced in slow motion in a video that looked as if it had been filtered through the same type of lens used to shoot each Barbara Walters special. On-screen titles in fonts designed to look like lace doilies introduced us to each "starring" member of the wedding party. As if I were watching some sort of wedding-themed horror movie, I didn't know whether to be sick or look away, and I watched the rest of the video through the space between my fingers to spare myself from the terrifying images unfolding on my TV screen.

Toward the end of our night, we watched one final video, and it came from a videographer whom we had contacted at the recommendation of a friend. The videographer's style was straightforward, almost journalistic, as if she made mini documentaries of each wedding she attended. Not needing fuzzy-bordered footage of the two of us dancing to adult-contemporary pop, Leora and I had found our videographer.

Of all the decisions you'll have to make about your wedding, don't get too hung up on this one. I believe that too many couples make themselves too stressed over picking a videographer without realizing that unlike your wedding photographs, which may be displayed in frames all over your home, your wedding video will probably spend most of its life in a closet or on a shelf, only to be shown on your anniversary or at the occasional family gathering. Your style may be completely different from mine and you may actually prefer cable-access-style graphics, but you probably share one sentiment: wedding videos are not that entertaining. You can't rent them at Blockbuster, you can't put them in your Netflix queue, and there's a reason the only wedding video you can find online is Pamela and Tommy's. At its best, yours will serve as video documentation of your wedding, something that future generations of kids and grandchildren will watch with minimal cringing.

ENGAGED GROOM TIP

But What I Really Want to Do Is Direct

Much of the cost of a videographer comes not from the four or five hours he or she spends shooting a wedding, but from the days or even weeks spent editing the footage. If you're looking to save money, ask your videographer if he or she will give you the raw, unedited footage. Even at the most exciting weddings, a videographer has to shoot hours of potentially sleep-inducing footage to get one hour of the best moments, so you may still want to edit it down. But with video editing software such as Apple's iMovie now bundled with most home computers, you may be able to save a few bucks by taking on this postwedding project yourself. Just make sure you have the right equipment at home, or the money you spend at the electronics store on upgrades may negate any savings you broker with your videographer.

To save even more money, why not skip hiring a videographer altogether? If you or someone you know has a camcorder, set it up on a tripod and let it run during the ceremony. Have your friends and family pass it around during the reception, or let different people record highlights of the event on their digital cameras, many of which have video modes. After your wedding, collect the footage from your friends and family and edit it together at home.

6

Choosing an Officiant

 Of course, none of your other wedding details—the food, the music, the pictures—will matter much if you don't have someone to marry you and your fiancée. More than anything, the person who performs your wedding will set the tone for your entire ceremony, and you'll undoubtedly want your wedding to be as personal as possible. Many couples, for that reason, tell their priest or rabbi about their plans to get married within days or even hours of telling their parents. And with good reason. Just as you wouldn't wait to hire an accountant until April 14, you should never wait too long to ask someone to perform your marriage, especially if you have a specific person in mind.

Religious officials, of course, are professionals just like anyone else and might well be booked solid during some of the year's busier wedding months. Factoring in important religious holidays and other observances, your priest or rabbi might simply not be available on the day you want to get married. This is especially true if you or your bride plan to use a childhood priest or rabbi with whom you haven't had much contact since your confirmation or bar mitzvah. As important as this person is to you or your bride, and as important as the two of you are to him or her, your house of worship is probably attended by hundreds of people, each with weddings, funerals, baby namings, and other events of their own.

When choosing a religious leader to perform your wedding, be sure to ask some basic questions, especially if you are approaching someone with whom you do not have a long history. Does he prefer that you get married in a house of worship or is he willing to perform a ceremony in a more secular setting? Do you have to be members of a church or temple to enlist the religious leader's services? Is there a fee for hiring the minister or rabbi or a suggested donation to the church or temple? If you and your fiancée follow different religions, will your minister or rabbi perform an interfaith ceremony? If you are both of the same faith, will your friends be allowed to participate in the wedding if they do not follow your religion's teachings? Many religions such as Catholicism have strict rules regarding divorce; if this is a second marriage for you or your fiancée, ask whomever you want to lead your ceremony if that will be a problem.

If you haven't been to a house of worship since your bar mitzvah or christening, you might be wondering how to find someone who can lead a religious ceremony. Just walking into a neighborhood church or synagogue is a good way to start, even if it might feel a little intimidating. If a particular religious leader is not available to perform your ceremony, he or she will probably be able to direct you to someone who is.

As it is with other wedding choices, asking friends who have recently been married for a recommendation is a good idea. They may be able to tell you some of the more personal details their officiant provided for their ceremony that you wouldn't have noticed as a spectator.

If you are taking a more civic route to your nuptials, you should be no less diligent in arranging an official to preside over your wedding. Check with your local county clerk's office or city hall to see what the procedure is for making an appointment with a justice of the peace. Many local government offices require that you pay a fee for using a state-sanctioned civic official, so call ahead to see that you are prepared for this small, but important, expense.

Many couples with judges or government officials in the family like to give them the honor of doing the honors. Just make sure the person you pick is eligible to do weddings in the place where you are getting married. The mayor of New York City, for example, can only perform weddings in New York City. Laws vary from state to state and from city to city, so do your homework to make sure that your officiant follows all legal requirements for performing weddings.

Some states have more lenient rules concerning who can perform weddings, provided that the person jump through a few bureaucratic hoops before asking you to repeat after him. In Massachusetts the person who leads your wedding ceremony need not be a religious official or justice of the peace. A friend or relative can preside over your wedding, but must obtain special permission from the governor's office. After being approved and paying a small fee, just about any legal adult can obtain a onetime special appointment to solemnize a marriage. California offers a similar option, granting what is essentially a one-day authorization for a friend or relative to perform a wedding.

If you do choose a friend or family member to lead your ceremony, take great care when making this decision. A rabbi or minister has probably performed hundreds or even thousands of weddings in his or her career and recognizes the deep solemnity of such an event. Same goes for a judge. Your uncle Sidney, however, might not know the finer points of marrying people and, no matter how much he loves you and your fiancée, could in fact be an entirely inappropriate choice. As far as I know, not too many religious officials or justices of the peace tell dirty jokes or embarrassing stories when marrying a couple. Experience breeds results, and you might not be satisfied with the results an inexperienced officiant brings to your ceremony.

One final note about a new, more modern twist on wedding officiants. You may have seen many Internet sites offering free or inexpensive online ordination. In fact, some of your friends may already have been certified by the Universal Life Church, the Spiritual Humanists, or some other Internet-based ordination service, simply by filling out an online form and clicking a box labeled ORDAIN ME. Only you will know whether this is a proper option for your wedding, but don't think that just because an obscure denomination or Internet-based church calls itself a religion that its ministers are authorized to perform weddings in your state. As with any choice you make, check the local requirements before choosing the person who will preside over an event as solemn, personal, and important as your wedding.

Part Two

THE FINER POINTS

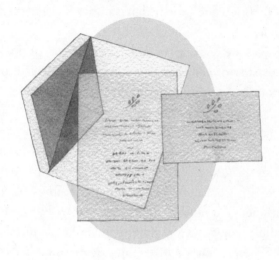

Now that you and your bride have taken care of some of the more pressing details, you'll probably have a chance to take a deep breath before taking care of some of the smaller details. This is when you'll start focusing on the real nitty-gritty, the things that will add individual style and personality to your wedding.

After the initial rush of picking a date, reserving a space, and, most notably, laying out a lot of cash in deposits and other fees, you might feel a tad overwhelmed. Take a few moments to orient yourself. Don't be concerned if a few of the larger pieces haven't fallen into place yet. Not every phone call will be returned exactly when you want it to be, and not every price quote will fall within your budget. You may have to go back to the drawing board more than once before things work out the way you want. The best-laid plans of bride and groom don't always happen exactly on schedule.

If you are starting to feel the strain of planning the biggest party of your life, you don't have to declare another moratorium on wedding planning, but remember to check in with your fiancée every so often. Cook dinner at home, go to a movie, take a weekend drive, or spend some time exploring a new neighborhood on the other side of town.

Over the next little while, you'll have a chance to involve even more people in your wedding planning. You'll pick groomsmen and other members of your wedding party, an incredible honor that any good friend or family member will readily accept. You'll start taking care of yourself by focusing on what you want to wear and heading to the designer tailor or discount superstore. You'll send out save-the-date cards, which will lead you one step closer to mailing invitations. Someone might throw you an engagement party or your bride might be the guest of honor at a wedding shower. Either way, you'll start registering for gifts, an activity that is a lot different—and hopefully more fun—than your normal trip to a department store. As if you didn't have enough to keep you busy before, here's where it starts to get *really* interesting.

7

Your Best Man
and Groomsmen

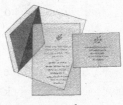 Unlike your fiancée's maid of honor
and bridesmaids, who traditionally at-
tend a number of prewedding festivities such as wedding showers and
dress fittings, the typical best man and
groomsmen have much shorter job descriptions. Living it up
at a bachelor party and ironing a clean shirt to wear under a
black tux are tasks even the least civilized men are glad to
handle.

Beyond having fun and dressing nicely, what are
groomsmen supposed to do? On your wedding day they
might serve double duty as ushers, escorting guests to their
seats so your ceremony can start on time. They might also
be your roadies in a sense, taking care of last-minute details
such as unrolling an aisle runner or dimming lights. More
or less, their job is to be on call before the ceremony to attend to you and offer you and your bride support on your
big day.

But despite the paucity of responsibility inherent in the

groomsmen's jobs, choosing the people who will stand by your side as you take your vows is a decision any Engaged Groom will want to take seriously. Even in a ceremony devoid of most religious traditions or rituals, your groomsmen will serve as spiritual witnesses to your marriage. The most cynical and jaded man will still feel honored to be given such an intimate role in your milestone event.

Depending on the size of your family and your circle of friends, selecting your groomsmen might feel like making draft picks for a Major League Wedding team. With your groomsmen serving as the starting lineup on your wedding day, you'll want the best bench possible to help you perform at your peak. But whereas a baseball manager can only field nine players and a basketball coach can only send five dribblers onto the boards, you are bound by no such restrictions. While I wouldn't recommend that you have fifteen groomsmen, I can't tell you to have only three.

What if you have five brothers and are nervous about picking one high school friend out of ten to fill a sixth spot? What if asking one member of your poker group to be a groomsman means having to ask the entire table? If you are concerned about bruised egos and hurt feelings, there are ways to set firm limits without offending anyone. One choice is to limit your groomsmen to family members. No one will blink an eye if you choose blood brothers over fraternity brothers. If you don't have enough family to round out your team, you can always extend offers to your bride's brother or cousins. But don't feel any pressure to pad the lineup; you don't have to have an equal number of groomsmen and bridesmaids no matter what anyone says. (Technically, you don't have to have any groomsmen at all. Some less formal weddings do away with the idea of bridesmaids and groomsmen altogether, and only the immediate family, religious or civil officiant, and bride and groom stand at the altar or under the chuppah.)

While your bride does not necessarily need to have final approval over your choices, I would not recommend making them in a vacuum. At this point in your relationship your bride probably knows your friends well, but that doesn't mean she gets along with all of them. You should be able to make a strong case for anyone you pick, but as an Engaged Groom you will of course be sensitive to your bride's opinions. After all, from where she's standing, your bride will have a pretty good view of everyone who's standing up with you.

MY BEST FRIEND'S WEDDING— THE BEST MAN'S JOB

Being a good best man is like being the cruise director on *The Love Boat*. He doesn't have to steer or plot the course, but it's his job to make sure all the passengers get on board and have a good time once the ship sets sail.

Before your wedding day your best man will most likely plan your bachelor party—if you choose to have one— making any dinner and entertainment reservations or travel arrangements for the bacchanal. He'll also serve as the liaison between you and your larger team of groomsmen. When everyone has to be fitted for tuxedos or other special uniforms in advance of your wedding, he's your point man. If you tell your best man everything you know about what to wear, where to wear it, and when to show up, a good one will pass this information along to everyone else so you don't have to worry about a thing.

Once your wedding day is under way, your best man might hang around when you get dressed. Not that you need anyone to help pull up your socks, but knowing that someone is around to check for a crooked tie or unzipped fly will give you a much needed added level of reassurance before the big event goes down. On the off chance you forget something big, like cuff links or your pants, you won't have to run around a hotel or church pantsless searching for any misplaced items. Like Robin to your Batman, a good friend will make sure you have all the gear you need on your wedding day.

But even though he's there to help you, every guy has his limits. Your best man isn't a fraternity pledge, intern, or military grunt. Don't abuse his generosity or take advantage of his goodwill, but don't be afraid to enlist him if your tuxedo needs to be sent for an eleventh-hour dry cleaning. The best kind of best man will do whatever it takes to ease your transition into married life.

What are his more specific responsibilities? He'll be there for any and all picture-taking sessions and will corral your groomsmen for formal portraits. He can hold your wedding rings during the ceremony and can be the caretaker of your wedding license after he signs it as an official witness. Traditionally the best man offers a toast at the reception, and a good one will strike the right balance between tasteful and tactless. (More on that later.)

Now that you know what the best man is supposed to do, who gets the job? There are no set rules for making such a decision, and no one who doesn't know your individual circumstances can give you an answer. If you have only one brother and are exceptionally close, your choice is probably a no-brainer. But what if you have two brothers or can't decide between your joined-at-the-hip college pals? Don't make a choice. It's that simple. There is no electoral college that will force you to send all your votes to one candidate. Having two best men and dividing the job responsibilities between two equally deserving contenders is the perfect solution, but remember each person's strengths and weaknesses. If your college roommate loves *Animal House*, let him plan the bachelor party while letting your more sensitive wordsmith brother serve up the perfect wedding toast. As for the choice of your groomsmen, this one's for you.

ENGAGED GROOM TIP

Gender-Bending the Rules

As with most wedding traditions, there isn't a ritual or practice that can't be changed to fit your specific situation. Therefore, there's nothing that says that your groomsmen technically have to be men. David, from Macon, Georgia, reached across gender lines when picking the people who would stand up with him at his wedding. "My best man was, well, a woman. I asked a good female friend of mine from college and beyond to do the honors."

Choices like David's are not uncommon. At my

wedding, my sister stood on my side with the honorary title of "best sister" and split some duties with my actual best man, a good friend from college. My sister wore a black dress to match my groomsmen's tuxedos. Having known my friends for almost as long as I knew them myself, she fit in perfectly and was more or less one of the guys. (Although not so much that she tagged along to the bachelor party. That would have been weird.)

FILLING OUT THE CAST—USHERS

As I mentioned before, your groomsmen may escort guests to their seats before your ceremony begins. But if you want to include even more people and give an honor to people without crowding the altar or chuppah, you can always ask them to be ushers. Although they need not wear the same thing as the groomsmen or even dress alike at all, as a courtesy all ushers should be given boutonnieres as a distinguishing marker for their special job. If you are having a small ceremony, you may find this to be overkill, since giving out too many honorary roles can mean that you have more people participating in the wedding than simply witnessing it. However, ushers can be quite helpful at larger gatherings and if you have any elderly guests who might need special assistance. If you're assigning ushers for a purely logistical purpose, have one for every fifty guests to make sure your guests find their seats in time for the ceremony to begin.

Friends Don't Let Friends Use Friends

I've never understood bridesmaids' dresses, and I would imagine that among Engaged Grooms I'm not alone. Why do so many brides force their friends to buy tacky, unflattering, and expensive dresses no more likely to be used again than a paper suit after a rainstorm? Fashion trends are shorter lived than most celebrity marriages, and I've been told that a bridesmaid's dress is dated as soon as a woman puts it on. So why do so many brides force their very differently shaped friends to try to fit into the same dress? Calling what would otherwise be a dress that no self-respecting woman would wear a "bridesmaid's dress" easily adds $100 to the price and means that women have to swallow their pride or risk offending the sensibilities of an otherwise well-meaning bride. Is this any way to treat friends?

That's not to say that grooms aren't also complicit in acts that could find them arrested for extortion in some jurisdictions. If you've ever had to rent a white dinner jacket for over a hundred bucks a night when you had a perfectly pressed classic black tuxedo hanging in a closet at home, you know what I mean.

Giving everyone a uniform look for pictures may be important to you and your bride, and that's fine. But if it's so important that you want every guy to buy an expensive designer tie and cummerbund set to match the bridesmaids' dresses, you may want to rethink your priorities. When you ask someone to participate in your wedding, you are asking that person to honor you, your bride, and your families by taking an active role in one of the most emotional and spiritual days of your lives. It's not a fashion show.

Leora, having been the victim of some fairly heinous and expensive bridesmaid's dresses chosen by some fashion-challenged friends, chose a different option for our wedding. Her only requirement was that her bridesmaids wear a below-the-knee dress within a palette of blues easy enough to find in all types of stores, from high-end houses of fashion to off-the-rack discounters. It was a win-win situation for everyone, as Leora told me that trying to find one dress that would flatter each of her friends' varying body types was a fool's errand. No one spent more money than they could afford, and most of the women picked their dresses with an eye on wearing them more than once.

My groomsmen, who were all over thirty years old, already owned tuxes. Did I care that one friend's tux had a shawl collar while the rest had peaked lapels? Not enough to make anyone rent a new one for the weekend. Leora and I had discussed having the groomsmen wear blue four-in-hand ties to match her bridesmaids' dresses, but decided it would be too expensive and told them to stick with the traditional black.

Leora and I followed a basic philosophy, neatly

summed up thusly: *friends are not props to be used in a wedding.*

After all, do movie producers ask actors to pay for their own costumes? If you insist on having your groomsmen wear matching ties, add the cost of purchasing them as a line item to your budget. If that is not possible, see if you can't at least offer some financial assistance by splitting the expense with your groomsmen or finding a cheaper alternative. Recognize that your friends are probably spending a lot of money simply to attend your wedding, and do your best to keep their costs as low as possible. Considering the amount of money they'll probably spend on your bachelor party and a gift, being sensitive to your friends' needs—not to mention avoiding any chance of pushing them into arrears with their credit card company or making them look ridiculous—is a defining characteristic of an Engaged Groom.

THANKSGIVING—GIFTS FOR GROOMSMEN

As a gesture of appreciation, it is customary for the groom to buy gifts for his groomsmen. Some grooms take the one-size-fits-all approach, buying the same thing for each of their friends, while others try to find more personal gifts to suit each groomsman's tastes. There's no right or wrong approach, but each has its advantages and disadvantages.

Buying the same gift for everyone, of course, saves time and, if done right, can still be meaningful. Gift certificates to a restaurant you all used to frequent as single guys might bring a tear to even your least-effusive pal. But even though most of your friends might appreciate an engraved flask or set of shot glasses, such a gift might not be so appropriate for your recovering-alcoholic brother-in-law. Nice wallets, engraved money clips, and Swiss Army knives are other types of gifts that cover many different types of guys.

Finding something different for each groomsman can be a challenge, but might be a great option if your friends are culled from many areas of your life and if you reach across gender lines when picking the people who will stand behind you. You might buy one gift for your college friends, another for your brothers, and still something different for your best friend from elementary school. The gifts can reflect their personalities, from the autographed football for the sports fan to a rare first edition for the book lover. Aside from the time it might take to hunt down individual gifts, the only other disadvantage might be that you wind up spending wildly different amounts on each one.

Of course, there's no reason why your groomsmen gifts have to be actual things at all. Feng shui fanatics and those who simply hate clutter might appreciate something less tangible. Take your groomsmen out to dinner once you're back from your honeymoon. Pick a night, reserve a block of tickets, and take your friends out to the ball game. For out-of-town groomsmen, a nice bottle of wine or a gift certificate to their favorite local music store might fit the bill.

Give your gift of thanks to your groomsmen at the rehearsal or rehearsal dinner before your wedding. You can make a public declaration of gratitude when presenting the gifts or you may prefer to do it during a more private moment.

Whatever you do, don't forget the ushers! For their role, it's perfectly appropriate to get them smaller tokens of your immense appreciation.

8

What to Wear and How to Look Your Best

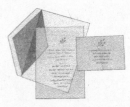

Being one-half of the center of attention means that there will be extra pressure to stand up straight, smile, and look not just good, but great. Whether it involves buying a new tux, spending a little more money on a stylish haircut, or worrying about losing the extra pounds you've packed on over the past few years, your engagement period and quickly approaching wedding are the perfect incentives for looking and feeling your best.

Since she'll be all dressed in white, it's easy for the bride to be the center of attention. But that doesn't mean that the attention is any less focused on the groom. Because they will soon find themselves scrutinized by every last friend and family member they've ever known, many guys feel a lot of pressure to focus on their appearance, something to which they might not have given much thought beyond the cursory look in the mirror before dashing off to work.

Suddenly, with the knowledge that you'll soon be standing at the front of a room and posing for dozens of pictures, even the smallest choices—cummerbund or suspenders?—can weigh heavily on a groom's mind. While your wedding day is of course the perfect opportunity for stepping up your normal fashion choices, don't get too hung up on sartorial details, and don't think that you have to be locked into a tuxedo or top hat and tails. It is perfectly acceptable to wear a suit at your wedding, and many less formal gatherings call for exactly that. It all depends on your overall style and comfort level and, of course, when and where you are getting married. In fact, a tux might not even be the right choice for you at all. Not too many people would choose to wear a suit made from black wool at a summer-afternoon wedding on the beach in Hawaii, but you never know.

ALL DRESSED IN BLACK—THE TUXEDO

Still, we should start with the basics, because that is most likely the place where you will start. Unless you are James Bond or work as a magician, you don't probably wear a tuxedo that frequently and may not be aware of the various styles. It's best to be as well versed as possible before confronting a salesperson or tailor in the men's department.

Despite the title of this section, don't get an image of head-to-toe black ensembles with only a white shirt peeking out from under a jacket. You can add some color by wearing a matching bow tie and cummerbund or waistcoat. More formal affairs might call for white tie and tails. A white dinner jacket is a classy option; it's typically worn with black pants, a white shirt, and a black tie. But that's about as big a departure as I would take from the black tuxedo. Powder blue tuxedos are good for costume parties and seventies-themed discos, but not for saying "I do."

Here are a few basic styles you should know about before slipping on a jacket:

JACKETS

More than any other piece of a tux, how a jacket fits is most affected by your weight, height, and body shape. Have you ever heard anyone say, "This bow tie makes me look fat?"

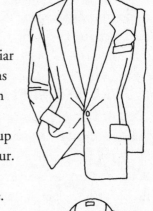

Single-breasted: This is probably the jacket most men are familiar with. It has one or two buttons in the front and looks good on just about anyone. If you are exceptionally tall, you might up the button total to three or four. Short or average-height guys, though, should stick with one.

Double-breasted: A misnomer of sorts, because the cut of this jacket overlaps more across your stomach. It has two rows of buttons on the front, one of which does nothing except look nice. The double-breasted jacket is often a better option for broad guys with a little more weight to them. David Letterman frequently wears a double-breasted suit on his show and never seems to know what to do with it when he's delivering his monologue.

Tailcoat: This is a jacket that's short in the front with two tails in the back. Wear this if you are having a very formal wedding and if you are above-average height. Short guys tend to look like penguins in this one.

Morning coat: Also called a cutaway coat, the front of this jacket gradually gives way to a wide tail in the back. More often than not, this jacket will be gray and is worn with an ascot. As the name implies, wear this at formal daytime weddings.

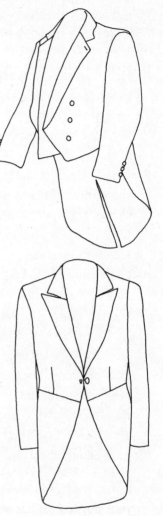

LAPELS

Your choices here are few, but give each one its due consideration. With a boutonniere attached to it, your lapel will get quite a lot of attention. (Remember, your boutonniere always goes on your left lapel.)

Notch: V-shaped cuts that point to where the collar and lapels meet are the distinguishing features of this lapel. A good choice for the skinny and/or tall.

Peaked: The points of this lapel shoot upward below where the collar comes to meet it. If you choose a peaked lapel, look for one where the peaks don't shoot out too far, or you'll look as if you could take off if you ran down a runway.

Shawl: Considered just a long collar more than a lapel, since it flows in a continuous line from around your neck to the midsection of the jacket. Shawl collars are almost always satin and look great on just about anyone.

SHIRT COLLARS

It might seem like we're getting into the nitty-gritty, but people will notice your shirt collar, especially in close-up photos. Here are the three most common types, two of which you are probably familiar with:

Turndown: Also called a laydown collar. You're already used to seeing this collar on the shirts you might wear with a suit to work. Somewhat informal, as far as collars go, but comfortable.

Spread: Similar to the turndown collar in just about every way, but the points of the collar aren't as acute. It's a more formal option that's favored by members of British royalty, of which you are probably not a descendant.

Winged: A common choice for tuxedos, this collar stands up straight around your neck but has small tips that point down. The shirt itself might also feature pleats down the front. The folded points should go behind your tie. Never rest them on top.

NECKWEAR AND TIES

Not every tie goes with every shirt and jacket and vice versa. Pick the tie that best matches the formality of your occasion and your outfit.

Ascot: Basically a scarf for your neck that is secured with a stickpin. Choose this option only for the most formal of weddings and wear it with a morning coat or tails. And also a monocle and top hat if you want to look like the guy from Monopoly.

Four-in-hand tie: Really, this is just your everyday necktie made from a more formal fabric. Tie it as you would any tie you might wear to work. Don't wear this with a cummerbund but instead pair it with a waistcoat, suspenders, or a belt.

Bow tie: The classic. Use a hand-tied tie if you can and a clip-on if you must, but know that the hand-tied option is considered classier. If you learn how to tie a bow tie now, you'll have a skill that will last you the rest of your life.

CLIP 'N' SAVE—
HOW TO TIE A BOW TIE

If you've never tied your own bow tie before, fear not! Use the instructions below and the illustration on the next page as your guide. Practice a few times and you'll be an expert on your wedding day!

1. Place the bow tie around your neck, so that end A is about two inches longer than end B.
2. Cross end A over end B.
3. Pull end A up and through the loop formed by the intersecting ends.
4. Double end B over itself. This forms the front base loop of the tie.
5. Loop end A over the center of the loop you just formed and let it hang.
6. Holding everything in place, double end A back on itself and push it through the loop behind the tie.
7. Adjust the tie by pulling gently at the ends. Straighten the center knot.

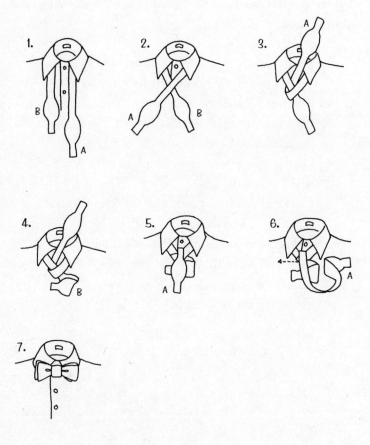

If you are still having trouble tying your bow tie, fold down the top of this page and hang it from a shirt pocket or from the waist of your pants. The reversed print will be readable in your mirror.

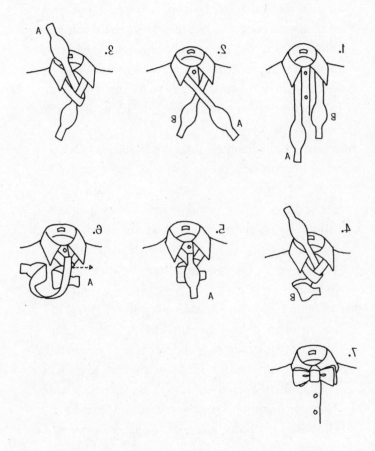

ACCESSORIZE—OTHER PARTS OF TRADITIONAL FORMAL WEAR

Cummerbund: If there were a contest to find the most useless piece of men's fashion, a cummerbund might win. Today, it does little more than look nice, but it once served a practical purpose for members of high society, holding theater tickets or money in its pleats. For that reason, and to live up to its nickname as a "crumb catcher," the pleats should be worn facing up.

Waistcoat: You'll definitely wear this if you choose a morning coat or white tie, but a waistcoat can be worn with less formal jackets as well. A waistcoat is essentially a small vest and is considered a step up from the cummerbund. The sheer number of fabrics, patterns, and colors in which waistcoats are available gives a man a mind-boggling amount of options.

French cuffs: This type of shirt has cuffs that roll back and are secured by cuff links. Heirloom cuff links from a parent or grandparent or a pair bought as a present from your bride are the way to go if you choose this classy option. You might also wear your personality on your sleeve, so to speak, by choosing cuff links in interesting shapes or colors.

Pocket square: A small piece of colored cloth that is
tucked into the left breast pocket of your jacket.
Chances are you won't wear this, as it is never seen
on a jacket with a boutonniere. If you do wear it,
it's not a handkerchief. Use a tissue for blowing
your nose.

Shoes: Patent leather shoes are standard-issue for most
tuxedos, but in many cases, a nice pair of black dress
shoes will suffice. Just remember to wear socks that
match your pants, and never, under any
circumstances, wear brand-new shoes to your
wedding. Take some time to break in your shoes, or
you'll be nursing two feet full of blisters on your
honeymoon.

THE GREAT DEBATE—RENT OR BUY?

If you already own a tuxedo and are getting good use out
of it at other events this year, you don't necessarily have to
upgrade to a newer, more expensive getup. You can save
money on the typical cost of buying or renting a tuxedo
by using what you have and dressing it up with a new
shirt, fancier cuff links, or a new tie and cummerbund set.
The price of any one of these items will be much less than
the cost of an entirely new tux and will make you feel like
just as much of a new man.

But what if your tux is starting to fray at the seams or if
you've lost a lot of weight in the race to the altar and think
it's worth the money to get married in something new?
What if you've never owned a tux at all and barely remem-

ber putting one on for your high school prom? You may have to make a decision: rent or buy?

Before you decide, think about the kind of formalwear you plan to wear at your wedding and the opportunities you'll have for wearing something like it in the future. The more formal your choice, the more sense it might make to rent, as the average guy probably attends few occasions that call for morning suits or tailcoats.

What about a white dinner jacket, a classy choice bound to distinguish you as the groom at your wedding? Unfortunately, a white jacket will also distinguish you at other events; in a sea of black jackets you're likely to stick out like an albino at a tanning salon.

Which brings us back to the traditional black tux. If you are getting married this year, chances are your friends or your fiancée's friends are, too, and you'll probably have a number of chances to wear your classic tux. Buying one of these, then, might make sense.

If you are on a crash diet for your wedding, renting might be a good option until you've decided that the weight you've lost is staying off. Spending hundreds or even thousands of dollars on a tux or suit that doesn't fit a few months after you wore it once would be a real waste. If you have to rent your tuxedo near your home and pack it for the trip to your destination wedding, the daily rental fee may wind up totaling more than the cost of one you can own outright.

ENGAGED GROOM TIP

No Sweat

Tuxedos and suits are the uniforms de rigueur for grooms of all shapes and sizes, no matter the season. But even if the weather outside is frightful, it can get a little toasty inside a black tux or wool suit, what with all the activity, dancing, and running around you'll do on your wedding day. Bigger guys or those with a tendency to sweat when they get nervous can find it a challenge to look their best hours into their wedding festivities. What's a self-conscious groom to do?

Buy two identical shirts, wear one during the ceremony, and then change into the fresh one before the reception. If you make it through the ceremony perspiration-free, you can still save the shirt for later. Sweatin' to the oldies can make even the best-looking groom smell a bit ripe.

THE BATTLE OF THE BULGE— DIET AND WORKOUT PLANS

Even the most stylish of cummerbunds can't conceal a pot-belly. This is not a workout guide, so don't look for any detailed pointers on sit-ups, crunches, and weight lifting, but there are some things to keep in mind if you're looking to shed a few pounds before your wedding day.

Between cake tastings and all of the parties that might be thrown in your honor, sticking to any diet plan can be daunting. The trick to any good weight-loss or workout plan, especially one with a looming deadline and lots of distractions, is to give yourself ample time to reach your goal. Trying to lose weight in the last few frenzied weeks before your wedding is a recipe for disappointment or worse. "Give yourself at least three months if you're serious about getting in better shape," says Patrick Panico, a physical trainer and strength and conditioning coach. "Anything less than that will just leave you hungry and possibly open to injury."

You don't necessarily have to join a pricey fitness center or hire a personal trainer if you're more comfortable being a couch potato than a gym rat. With enough regularity, brisk after-work walks, quick bike rides, or twenty-minute jump-rope sessions can be just enough to mean the difference between having your pants taken in and looking for extrastrength suspenders.

Make your weight loss a challenge among your friends. Mike, a Web programmer from Brooklyn, New York, made a bet with his groomsmen, all of whom wanted to shed a few pounds. They each picked a target weight, and anyone who did not reach it by Mike's wedding would pay $500 into the pool. The money was then divided among those who were successful. You don't have to pledge half your rent to the effort, but adding a competitive element to your weight-loss goals might just be the incentive you need.

One warning: don't make your weight loss a challenge between you and your fiancée. It's a surefire way to wind up in a fight. Discussions of weight and dieting can be awkward even among the most open and honest couples.

9

Save-the-Date Announcements, Invitations, and Getting the Word Out

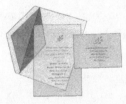

If a wedding happens in a secluded church and no one knows about it, will anyone come? The fact is, no matter how big or small your wedding will be, you have to get the word out somehow. In an age of e-mail, instant messaging, and cell phones, spreading the news should be easy. But weddings are nothing if not highly traditional affairs, and your event may call for more than just a mass e-mail or a posting on Evite. E-mails, after all, get lost or deleted easily, and some might even wind up blocked by a computer's spam filter. No, for an event as important as your wedding, you'll want to start familiarizing yourself with something you might not have used in a long time: the good ole United States Postal Service.

PENCIL IT IN—SAVE-THE-DATE ANNOUNCEMENTS

The sensibly named save-the-date announcement does exactly what you would expect. It alerts your guests that you are getting married and advises them to—now stay with me here—save the date. The standard save-the-date announcement is traditionally sent approximately six months before the wedding, but if your event will involve complicated travel or is scheduled for a notoriously busy holiday weekend, I would suggest mailing your save-the-dates as much as eight months in advance. Even if you're having a local affair with mostly in-town guests, giving your friends and family adequate advance notice will help ensure that everyone who wants to be at your wedding will be. (If you just read the preceding and are in a panic because you have less than six months until your wedding day, don't worry. In a crunch, four months should still give people enough time to clear their calendars.)

Save-the-date announcements can take many forms and need not be formal at all. In fact, many couples use the save-the-date announcement as a place to show off their personalities and interests and use everything from creative photographs to illustrated maps as a design. Magnets with a couple's names, the wedding date, location, and a photograph or design have become popular in recent years and, since they immediately get stuck on your guests' refrigerators, are not easily lost. Whatever you choose, you don't have to spend half your printing budget on a mini-invitation with embossed lettering or calligraphy. Leora and I made our save-the-date letters on our home computer and had them printed at a local copy shop for less than $50. Postal rates being what they are, it cost more to mail them.

What should your save-the-date announcement say? Some couples send simple postcards covering only the bare necessities:

Save the Date!

Leora and Doug are getting married!

Sunday, August 29th, 2021
Oconomowoc, Wisconsin

Invitation to follow

Other couples, knowing that their guests might appreciate more information for their globe-spanning trips, send more detailed announcements or include a short letter with any card they send. If you're planning to have more than one event, such as a brunch or rehearsal dinner, over your wedding weekend, include a schedule with your save-the-date or write a letter describing your plans so your guests will know they are invited for more than just the wedding. Such a letter might begin with a more general greeting:

Dear friends and family,

We're looking forward to sharing our wedding with you in Oconomowoc, Wisconsin, on Sunday, August 29th, 2021. We'd love to see you for the entire weekend, so please join us Friday through Sunday for all of the events we have planned.

The letter should include all pertinent information on hotels, airlines, and car rental companies, including phone numbers, Web addresses, and any codes necessary for booking specially reserved rooms and discounted fares. ("Mention the Kaye-Gordon wedding when making your reservation," for example.) You might also include driving directions or a map. Other details such as the typical weather for the time of year where you are getting married, a suggested packing list ("The hotel is on a beach, so bring a bathing suit, sunblock, and your surfboard"), and a rundown of local tourist attractions will also help your guests plan their trips. Many of my friends, born-and-bred Northeasterners, wanted to see more of the Midwest than just Oconomowoc, Wisconsin, and extended their stays to include side trips to Chicago and other points of interest.

If you are having a destination wedding in a foreign country, alert your guests to any travel restrictions or visa requirements. (Although I wouldn't recommend choosing a destination that requires your guests to get a series of immunizations for malaria or yellow fever.)

Don't forget to include your home phone number or your parents' contact information on your save-the-dates. No matter what information you include, your guests will inevitably have a lot of questions. You'll minimize any potential confusion if you and your bride, your parents, and her parents have the proper information for handling all inquiries.

One final and important note about save-the-date announcements: they are, in effect, preliminary wedding invitations and cannot be revoked. Anyone on your guest list when the save-the-date cards are mailed should still be on it when the invitations are sent. You can always send an invitation to someone who did not receive a save-the-date, but it's poor form to cross someone off your list once he's already essentially been invited to your wedding.

ENGAGED GROOM TIP

The World Wide Wed

Posting information about your wedding online is an easy way to keep even the most absentminded friends and relatives informed of everything they'll need to show up in the right place at the right time. I've lost plenty of wedding invitations in my life, but so far I've never lost a computer.

Even if you're a stubborn Luddite and the thought of diving into HTML programming gives you nightmares of pale-skinned computer geeks, fear not. Plenty of companies are more than happy to do the heavy lifting by building your Web site for you . . . for a fee, of course.

Many hosting providers dedicated to the art of wedding Web sites offer design and construction packages, typically in twelve-month increments with additional months available for more money. Some may even offer you your own domain name. Of course, with millions of couples getting married each year, getting the one you want might be tricky. Even though my first name is common, my wife's isn't, so the chances of www.dougandleora.com being taken is slim at best. But if your name is John or David and your bride's name is Mary or Amy, you might have to get creative.

Your Web site should feature the same information you'll include in a save-the-date announcement and can even be an enhanced multimedia version of your mailing. Provide links to hotels and airlines, pictures of the venue where your ceremony is being held, and even a wedding journal to keep your guests up-to-date on all the planning. Some companies offer an online RSVP option for your guests, but most couples still prefer the old-fashioned printed response card, a tradition I suspect is unlikely to fall victim to the digital age. Information about your gift registry can be included on your wedding Web site, although it should be done discreetly; don't put up any banner ads across the top of your site linking to a department store.

Of course, if your Web site will be used mainly

for informational purposes, you might not need to pay for something with a lot of bells and whistles. There is plenty of free online real estate available, and your very own ISP may offer packages that include free Web hosting. For the Engaged Groom who is confident in his programming abilities, this might be the perfect option. WeddingChannel.com is also a popular site for much of your wedding needs, and offers free space for posting information about your wedding and gives you the ability to link various gift registries in one convenient location.

A note of caution: because of the public nature of the Internet and given that etiquette standards have not yet been established online, you may want to consider making your Web site password-protected. You probably don't have to worry about strangers crashing your wedding, but keeping your site under lock and key is a safe way to draw a clear line between invited guests and your merely curious officemates or ex-girlfriends.

SIGNED, SEALED, DELIVERED—INVITATIONS

Of all the wedding tasks, none can seem as big as getting invitations printed, addressed, and ready for mailing. Some couples look at a few proofs, write up a guest list, and push the task off onto wedding planners, stationers, and calligraphers. But if you are taking a more hands-on approach and will be licking more than a few envelopes yourself, you might have a few questions.

When should you have your invitations printed? Start this soon, as you'll need a fair amount of time before your wedding day to make sure you get everything printed, addressed, and posted in time. A lead time of three to four months should do the trick. Any longer than that and you'll increase the risk of encountering a problem that could send your expensive invitations to the paper shredder. You'd probably hate to have hundreds of invitations printed that list a five o'clock reception only to have the country club call you to tell you that they made a mistake and are booked until six.

How many invitations should you have printed? Not as many as you might think. Take a look at your guest list, then do some subtraction. Couples and families need only one invitation per household, not one per person. A 200-person guest list might mean an actual mailing of only 125 invitations or fewer. But as a precaution against invitations that get lost in the mail, order approximately twenty-five extras. If you are sending out invitations to a B-list (see the tip on B-lists later in this chapter), make sure you have enough on hand to cover this group. Most printing companies require a minimum of 100 invitations per printing, so waiting to order extras until you need them can be not only expensive, but wasteful as well.

What should they say? While you may have gotten creative with your save-the-date announcement, some couples feel that their wedding invitation should strike a more formal tone. Here's the traditional wording for an invitation to a wedding hosted—read "largely paid for"—by the **bride's**

parents that takes place at a house of worship and is followed by a reception in a different location:

Mr. and Mrs. Gerard W. Kaye
request the honour of your presence
at the marriage of their daughter
Leora Rachel
To
Mr. Douglas Aaron Gordon
Sunday, the twenty-ninth of August
Two thousand and twenty-one
at five o'clock
Temple Emmanuel
123 Main Street
Oconomowoc, Wisconsin

Reception following

Note the British spelling of the word *honour*. You may not be able to trace your lineage to King George III, but such usage is common on formal wedding invitations.

Some couples prefer to put information about the reception on a separate, smaller card or with an enclosed response card, but this can add to your printing costs. (See the next section for more information on response cards.)

If your wedding won't take place in a house of worship, you can shorten the wording above. You might also take out the phrase "honour of your presence" and replace it with "favour of your company" or "pleasure of your company" if you are getting married at a country club or more secular location. (Real sticklers for tradition will tell you that it is an honor to attend a religious ceremony, and jokers will tell you that sitting on uncomfortable wooden pews for an hour is anything but a pleasure.)

What if **your parents** are hosting the wedding? Your invitation might look like this:

> **Mr. and Mrs. Neil R. Gordon**
> **request the honour of your presence**
> **at the marriage of**
> **Miss Leora Rachel Kaye**
> **to their son**
> **Douglas Aaron Gordon**

No matter who is hosting the wedding, it is customary for the bride's name to be listed before the groom's.

Invitation wording can be as varied as families themselves. Your parents or your bride's might be divorced or one of them might be widowed. Your father may be a doctor and you may be serving as an officer in the marines. If so, use your professional titles. Your future mother in-law might go by her maiden name and hates being referred to as Mrs. Her Husband's Name. Perhaps both of your families are splitting the expenses fifty-fifty. Ultimately, the wording you'll choose will reflect the economic and familial realities of your wedding. Plenty of online resources as well as classic etiquette books from domestic doyennes such as Emily Post offer example after example to fit family trees of every shape and size.

Family concerns and a regard for pretense and tradition might not even be a factor in your decision at all. If **you and your bride** are hosting everything yourselves and prefer a lighter tone, you might choose to word your invitation as follows:

> **Leora Rachel Kaye**
> **and**
> **Douglas Aaron Gordon**
> **invite you to celebrate with us**
> **at our wedding**

As with any wedding tradition, the examples I included above are customary, not mandated. Use whatever wording you like as long as the information is clear and easy to understand. Plenty of other examples exist online, but there's an even better resource probably available to you almost weekly: other people's wedding invitations. Take a look at the ones you have received recently and see if someone else's wording has seemed exceptionally classy or creative.

There's one last question that everyone has about invitations, and it is, of course, the most important one of all: When do they go out? In most cases, your invitations should be mailed six to eight weeks before your wedding date. If you did not send a save-the-date or are concerned about guests who will have to make extensive travel plans, then a ten-week lead is not unusual.

The Separation of Church and Crate (& Barrel)

No Engaged Groom wants to give the impression that he's using his wedding to stock his home or apartment with shiny new stuff. Your bride probably feels exactly as you do. For that reason, the biggest invitation faux pas and the one most likely to draw the silent ire of your guests is to include information about your registry on your invitation. You shouldn't even put registry information on a printed card or piece of paper included in the same envelope as your invitation. You're inviting people you know to your wedding, right? Presumably those people will know you or your families enough to ask where they can buy you a gift.

RETURN TO SENDER— RESPONSE CARDS

Traditional wedding invitations include a small response card on which guests can indicate their intent to attend your wedding or, for whatever reason, can decline your invitation. For more formal invitations, a small stamped envelope should be included with the response card so that your guests can mail the cards back as quickly and easily as possible. If you need to consider a less expensive option, eliminate the envelope and have your response cards labeled like small postcards. This will help you save money not only on printing, but also on postage.

The parents of the bride, as the traditional hosts of a wedding, are the point people for tracking attendance, and any response cards or envelopes should be preprinted with their home address. Your situation might warrant a different approach, either because you or a different part of the family is hosting the wedding or because one set of parents lives in a foreign country where mail is delivered by camel, raft, and Sherpa and takes six months to reach its destination.

Your response deadline should be three to four weeks before the wedding. That means that if your invitations are sent out six to eight weeks before the wedding, your guests will have only three to four weeks to respond. This deadline is meant to give you time to finalize details with caterers and other vendors for whom a hard number of guests is a vital piece of information. It also gives you a tiny window during which to track down delinquent responders. (More on that later.)

A simple way to format a response card is as follows:

Kindly respond by the first of August

M _____

will _____ attend the wedding

For a more personal touch, some couples send a card that simply lists the response deadline over a field of blank space. This option offers your guests the chance to write a note in which they might express either their immense joy for the chance to celebrate with you or their feeble excuses for why they'll have to miss your wedding.

Whichever style you choose, keep your response cards as information-free as possible. A simple deadline date and polite request to reply is all you need. You might have seen response cards printed with reception details, such as the time and location. But this makes little sense. Once the card is dropped in a mailbox, how will your guests be able to remember where to show up for the party?

As simple as they seem to be, many guests get confused by response cards. Call it a sign of the times. With online invitations so commonplace for other minor events, your friends may be a tad out of practice when it comes to sending in a formal RSVP. Don't be surprised if you receive cards that are mysteriously left blank or that are simply marked with an X between "will" and "attend." To prepare for this inevitability—and trust me, it is inevitable—use a light pencil to write a number on the back of each response card that corresponds to a number in your wedding-guest database. If a card comes back lacking a name or is written in illegible chicken scratch, you'll know whom to contact for a translation.

OTHER INFORMATION

Beyond the basic details of who, what, where, and when, what other information goes on your invitations? The dress code can be printed at the bottom beneath the reception information, and "Black Tie" is a common notation for formal affairs. Other terms, however, might confuse your guests, and if you are having a more casual party, "Festive Attire" or "Casual Dress" does little to tell them what to pack. Should they wear suits and cocktail dresses or Halloween costumes and leather pants? For that reason, some couples choose to leave information about what to wear off the invitations altogether and either include a note in the save-the-date announcement or make calls to friends and family with more specific details.

If you are having a sit-down dinner with a choice of entrées, you might ask your guests to note their preference for, say, beef or fish on the response card in advance. Some people consider this horribly low-rent, but remember that you are throwing a party, not opening a restaurant. Having enough food on hand to allow guests to make an either-or decision at your party is nice, but it adds a huge expense to the catering bill. Asking guests for their orders in advance can prevent you from having to pay for one hundred pieces of unused salmon when everyone at your party orders the steak.

SEEK 'N' SPELL—PROOFREADING YOUR SAVE-THE-DATES AND INVITATIONS

Perhaps the most important and overlooked part of printing wedding invitations is having them proofread for spelling and accuracy. Printers are not mind readers, and even the best ones make spelling mistakes. But as any stationer worth his weight in card stock or vellum will probably tell you, such mistakes are usually the fault of the people ordering the invitations and not the person manning the presses.

Names, of course, should be proofread, especially if you or your fiancée has a unique name or an unusual way of spelling a common name. Check all dates so that your guests don't show up at the church or temple one day early, and make sure all other information such as addresses and phone numbers is correct as well. A second set of eyes isn't enough. Pass a proof of your invitation and all other printed material around to your parents, your bride's parents, and other family members as well. An impartial set of eyes is always a good idea, as someone with a little more distance might see things that a close member of the family takes for granted.

I can't stress enough the importance of proofreading. On our save-the-dates, we accidentally switched two digits of the phone number of one of the hotels at which we had booked a block of rooms. Luckily we caught the mistake before we repeated it with our invitations, but this caused no small amount of confusion for our guests. It also caused an incredible amount of hassle for poor Mr. and Mrs. Hatch of Oconomowoc, Wisconsin, who had to explain over and over that, no, you had not reached the Lake Country Inn.

ENGAGED GROOM TIP

Some Assembly Required

The average wedding invitation involves no fewer than four separate pieces: the invitation itself, the response card, the envelope for the response card, and the larger envelope in which everything is mailed. Many invitations may involve even more pieces, such as an inner envelope within the mailing envelope and small printed cards with driving directions and hotel information. Printing companies not only will charge you for printing each piece, but will also charge a fee for putting everything together.

To save money, put the invitations together at home, but be prepared; this is no small task. Assembling two hundred invitations can easily involve between six hundred and one thousand separate pieces, so don't go it alone. Invite the future in-laws over with your parents and have everyone grab a stack. When you're done, thank everyone for contributing to your do-it-yourself thriftiness by paying for dinner.

PLEASE, PLEASE, MR. POSTMAN— WHAT THE STAMPS ON YOUR INVITATIONS SAY ABOUT YOU

In your normal, everyday life, you don't usually give much thought to what kind of stamps you use. You stick a stamp on an envelope, drop it in the mail, and it is easily delivered to its intended address. But if you've learned nothing else so far, you know that nothing is normal when your life is focused on wedding planning.

If your bride or someone in your family is obsessed about paper stocks, color schemes, and fonts, is it really such a jump to believe that someone might think that picking the right stamps is just as important as anything else? But before you or your bride go postal standing in line to buy just the right stamps for your invitations, ask yourself, does anyone really notice the postage? In the history of the English language, I guarantee you no one has ever opened their mail and said, "What a lovely invitation, but, man, check out that ugly stamp."

Still, if such things are important to you, you can buy packages of stamps designed for wedding invitations that feature bouquets of flowers. There are even stamps that celebrate love itself, but with your wedding set to be endorsed by a religious officiant and the state or states in which you will be married and reside, you don't necessarily have to let the postmaster general issue his stamp of approval as well.

You might think flowers or candy hearts are a little too, for lack of a better word, girly, while your bride might think that an American flag or stamp bearing the image of a historical figure isn't wedding-centric enough, as patriotic as you both may be. As a compromise, why not make your own stamp? As of this writing, Stamps.com allows you to upload your own pictures to create "photo stamps" in various first-class rates for your personal use. Putting a smiling picture of you and your fiancée on each invitation sounds cute, but I'm not sure how I'd feel about using the extras to mail a phone bill.

While you're weighing your choices, don't forget to weigh your actual invitations. A heavyweight or oddly sized envelope may require additional postage. Invitations intended for overseas guests will have to be posted separately, and don't forget to affix the proper postage to response cards and return envelopes so that your guests' RSVPs can find their way back home.

KEEPING TRACK OF IT ALL

Once your invitations have been mailed, it won't take long before the responses start pouring in. No matter who is in charge of keeping the master list, make sure that person is prepared. If you are having a small wedding, tracking responses from forty guests is probably no more challenging than seeing who's free for dinner on a Saturday night. If you are mailing hundreds of invitations, however, keeping track of every person's response can seem a little daunting.

Before the responses pile up in someone's mailbox, prepare the spreadsheet in which you are keeping the master guest list for its new job as a response tracker. Insert a new column with the heading "RSVP." If you have events in addition to the wedding, such as a rehearsal dinner, you can label each column with the name of each event: "Wedding" and "Rehearsal Dinner," for example. With each response that comes in, mark the column row next to each person's name with a *Y* for yes and an *N* for no. You'll easily be able to sort your data to see who's coming, who'd rather be doing something else, and who hasn't responded yet.

OUR GUEST LIST

LAST NAME	FIRST NAME	STREET ADDRESS
Anderson	Nicholas and Marita	91 Eagle Pond Road
Bennett	Leigh and Scott	625 College Avenue
Birnbaum	Amy and Adam	1089 Peachtree Road
Boxt	Jason and Rosalie	456 Monument Avenue
Cunningham	Lew, Moira, Zach, and Zoe	20 Hannah Lane
Gordon	Kenneth, Dara, Michael, and Laura	10 Maple Hill Terrace
Gordon	Miriam	28 Royal Crest Street #5
Hirschfield	Irene and James	507 Park Avenue
Hirschfield	Jordan and Jody	348 Elm Street
Lerner	Sidney and Blossom	621 Summer Terrace Lane
Mates-Muchin	JT and Jacqueline	7031 Oceanview Drive
Perry	James	890 Commonwealth Avenue #1L
Rigler	Peter and Stacey	305 East 24th Street #3R
Silverman	Alan and Michelle	26 Prospect Place

ENGAGED GROOM TIP

Enter the Matrix?

In your travels through the wilds of wedding planning, you've probably encountered a number of ad-

CITY	STATE	ZIP CODE	WEDDING	REHEARSAL
New London	NH	03255	Y	Y
Dallas	TX	75201		
Atlanta	GA	30301	N	N
Washington	DC	20008	Y	Y
Newton	MA	02141	Y	N
Larchmont	NY	10539		
Andover	MA	01812	Y	Y
St. Louis	MO	63101		
St. Louis	MO	63102		
Glen Rock	NJ	07458	Y	Y
Oakland	CA	94601	Y	Y
Boston	MA	02144	N	N
New York	NY	10036	Y	N
Milwaukee	WI	53209	N	N

vertisements extolling the virtue and value of wedding planning software. With the same skeptical eye you might reserve for fending off snake oil salesmen, don't let anyone convince you to order software designed to plan your wedding. I found one Web site selling software with the claim that it will make keeping track of everything from addresses to thank-you notes easier "whether you are inviting 100 or 1,000 people." One thousand people? Who is the target audience? J. Lo?

Any software package that claims to make the planning easier or to give you complete control over the wedding details is selling you a bill of goods. Not even the most sophisticated computer program can deal with a hyperactive sibling, meddling mother-in-law-to-be, or stubborn father, the very people who often want to wrestle control away from a helpless bride and groom. Unless it comes with two tickets to Vegas and wedding cake mix to which you just have to add water, no software package can give you and your fiancée complete control over anything.

Typically there isn't anything in these computer programs that you or your fiancée don't already have or can't easily make yourself. In fact, many are little more than flowery pink versions of Excel or a similar program you already use at home or in the office. The information on such programs usually consists of checklists and schedules that are either so obvious that they hardly need explaining or so comprehensive that you'd need an engagement period of ten years and five weddings to follow every last detail. At the end of the day, much of what you will find in wedding planning software is freely available elsewhere online, in print, and from friends.

DON'T TAKE MAYBE FOR AN ANSWER

Some guests might tell you that they are a maybe, and that they'll have to give you a more definitive response after your RSVP deadline. I would advise against letting people sit on the fence for too long. You have a large event to plan and will have to provide hard numbers to a caterer so he or she can order food, and you won't have time to get definitive answers out of those who have a hard time making decisions. However, as an Engaged Groom you'll certainly consider any circumstances that may render prompt and specific RSVPs impossible. A cousin awaiting top-secret military deployment and a friend in med school awaiting his unpredictable hospital rotation schedule may deserve special consideration regarding your hard-and-fast deadlines.

ENGAGED GROOM TIP

To B-list or Not to B-list?

On its surface, a B-list seems like such a simple idea. You want to invite 220 guests but can only afford to host 210, so you send invitations to all but those last ten people. For every regret that comes in, you send a new invitation to the next person on your B-list. If you're pressed for space or money, a B-list can be a way to include the people you might otherwise be unable to invite.

I think that having a B-list creates more problems than it solves, but that's just me. On top of everything else Leora and I had to do, remembering to send out a second or third batch of invitations after the initial round would just have been one more item on our already long to-do list. Still, some people are more than willing to do the extra work, and as long as you can keep track of your schedule and responsibilities, go for it.

The ugly truth, however, is that having a B-list is a potential Pandora's box of problems and hurt feelings. Why? Because unless you are a master of organization, it's easy for people to figure out if they didn't make the first cut. With dozens or even hundreds of invitations hitting people's mailboxes at once, it won't take long for someone to realize why he hasn't received one, especially as your wedding day draws closer. And even if a spot does open up at the last minute, an invitation received less than one month before the wedding is a surefire sign of not making the A-team. A person who figures out he's been B-listed might resent it more than if he had never been invited at all. Additionally, creating a B-list is never as simple as making a list of ten extra people you'd like to invite and then ticking them off one by one. What happens if you don't make it all the way through your list? Will you be comfortable inviting the eighth person on your B-list but not the ninth and tenth?

A firm cutoff and a policy of honesty is, in my opinion, the best solution. If someone is disappointed about not receiving an invitation, you are free to offer your apologies. You don't have to show a bank statement or your financials; any reasonable person will understand the economic reality that influenced your decision and may ultimately be happy not to have to take his tuxedo out of storage. Besides, anyone who would hold such a choice against you is probably not deserving of an invitation to your wedding in the first place.

PROBLEM GUESTS

The best-laid plans of bride and groom will always be complicated by the most unpredictable variable in all of wedding planning: other people. Under no circumstances would I want to scare you, but you should, at least, be duly warned. In some cases, not until after the invitations have gone out do the problems start.

As an Engaged Groom, you already know to be sensitive to the varied needs of your guests. That doesn't mean you have to honor all requests, as some can actually be downright preposterous. For example, that you are serving food often makes guests think they are going to a restaurant with special menus to accommodate every diet, taste, and appetite. "One guest wrote on his response card that if we were serving beef, he would like his well done, and if we were serving fish, he would like the vegetarian meal, and if we were serving chicken, he would like it plain with lemon and butter," says one anonymous groom.

Some requests range from the ridiculous to the supremely ridiculous. "A friend asked if we could move our Sunday-afternoon wedding to a Saturday night," says Jordan from Austin, Texas. "In all seriousness, she had to be at work early on Monday and wanted to be able to drink at the party. I decided to answer her with sarcasm and said, 'Sure. Let me check with the one hundred and seventy-four other people we invited.'"

It's hard to say in advance which guests will cause the most aggravation, and you may be lucky not to face any at all. Regardless, here's a heads-up and a rundown of the most common problem guests:

The Late Responder: Remember that *RSVP*, from the French for *Répondez s'il vous plaît,* translates to "Respond, *if you please.*" Unfortunately, some guests take this literally and choose not to send in their response cards by the deadline . . . or even at all. If this happens, feel free to call these delinquent responders and politely ask about their status. While dealing with someone who thinks the rules apply to everyone but him might really stick in your craw, you don't have to be a stickler for formality; if he insists on phoning in his reply, kindly take his information, make a note of it on your guest list, and move on.

The Overprotective Parent: Some guests might wonder if their children are invited, and the answer is simple. If an invitation is addressed to Kenneth and Dara Gordon, only its recipients, Kenneth and Dara, are invited. If it had been meant to convey an invitation to their children, it would have included their children's names on the envelope or been appended with "and Family." You may already have decided to limit kids to those belonging to immediate family members, so be consistent if you decide to make any exceptions. And be clear with any family members who you think may bring their kids anyway. Jake and Lori, from New York, New York, had a bit of a problem with this. "We were a bit blown away by the audacity of guests who brought children who were not invited. Why people thought it was okay to bring people whose names were clearly not on the envelope was beyond us. What's worse is that the people whose children weren't invited and were smart enough not to bring them looked a little slighted. Who can blame them?" (As an Engaged Groom you should be sensitive to even the most overprotective parent; if your wedding will take place out of town, offer to help find qualified babysitters in the area.)

The Meddler: Occasionally, even the best-intentioned friend or family member can cause the biggest headaches for you and your bride. In fact, my experience has taught me that the person who says, "I'm just trying to make things easier for you," will probably wind up doing the exact opposite. With all that you and your bride have to do, you might appreciate an extra pair of hands, but more likely than not it will just be easier to keep everything on a tight leash. If a friend insists on helping, either give him an unimportant task he can't possibly screw up or politely tell him that the only thing you need is for him to enjoy himself at your wedding. Most people will take the hint.

The Complainer: After our invitations went out, one of my friends complained about the location. This person made her dissatisfaction known at every available opportunity, complaining about having to arrange travel and asking us why we weren't having the wedding in New York even though she knew Leora's family was from the Midwest. Unable to hide my annoyance after another of her tirades, I couldn't take it anymore. "I hope that when you find the person you're going to marry," I said, "that he is from somewhere that's convenient *for me*." With that, the person stopped complaining and wound up having a great time at our wedding, or so I was told.

Wedding attendance is never mandatory. If someone has a problem with your plans, they should either put their feelings on the back burner out of respect for you and your bride or find a more sensitive way to talk about them.

READ ALL ABOUT US—ENGAGEMENT AND WEDDING ANNOUNCEMENTS

Whether you think it's quaint or feel strongly that the practice reeks of high-society snobbery, many newspapers print engagement or wedding announcements. You've probably given little or no thought to a section of the paper frequently nicknamed Mergers & Acquisitions or, more stereotypically, the Female Sports Pages. Even if you have been known to flip through the society pages to see if you recognize anyone, it's still a safe bet that your bride or future mother-in-law will have the final say on whether you submit an announcement.

Printing news of your engagement is not without risk. If you are a particularly private couple, making such a public declaration can open you up to scrutiny. The Weddings/Celebrations section of the *New York Times*, for example, has provided fodder for at least two episodes of *Sex and the City* and is the target of more than a few snarky bloggers' barbs.

The effects of announcing your wedding plans in a major newspaper may be felt closer to home. After reading about your engagement, everyone from long-lost friends to distant relatives might crawl out of the woodwork asking for an invitation. Some papers, however, provide a safety net of sorts. With many engagements getting called off before the wedding, an increasing number of papers have ceased featuring such notices altogether, waiting instead until couples have legally sealed the deal. The *New York Times*, for example, publishes a weekend's worth of weddings in the back of their Sunday Styles section, but does not announce engagements.

Knowing the pitfalls and perils of public wedding announcements, what should yours say if you decide to go ahead and submit one anyway? A typical announcement includes the names of the bride and groom, their hometowns, their educations, professions, and similar information for their parents. It also notes the location of the ceremony and the name and affiliation of the presiding religious or civil official. Some papers may also include a brief story noting how the bride and groom first met. If you are widowed or divorced, they might also print that information.

Your local paper may print a picture to run with your announcement and most likely has specific rules and requirements for submitting photos. The *New York Times* requests that pictures be set "at home, outdoors, or in other attractive settings," which most likely means you shouldn't submit a picture taken in front of a McDonald's. The *Times* also asks that brides and grooms "arrange themselves with their eyebrows on exactly the same level with their heads fairly close together," making it sound as if you might need an engineer to properly set up your picture. In the mother of all throwbacks, some papers only print a picture of the bride, sometimes in her full wedding regalia. You may find this not just anachronistic, but sexist, too.

If you and your fiancée decide to announce your wedding in a local paper, check the paper's Web site or call their editorial office for all requirements and send everything in six to eight weeks before your wedding day. But due to the high volume of submissions, even following the rules and meeting deadlines is no guarantee that you'll be included. There are only a limited number of pages in even the biggest newspapers, and the competition can be fierce. So fierce, in fact, that some papers employ a team of fact checkers to weed out wannabes. For our announcement, a reporter asked Leora to fax a copy of her college transcript to show that she did, in fact, graduate from the University of Wisconsin. The paper didn't ask for a DNA test or urine sample, but considering the value some people place on having their announcement printed, that day can't be far off.

In one notable case, the *New York Times* had to run a correction after it was discovered that a woman who in her wedding announcement claimed to have earned a Ph.D. in neuroscience actually only held a bachelor's degree. Who knows if her claims of higher education helped her announcement pass muster with the *Times'* editors, but it's pretty foolish to assign yourself a degree two levels above what you actually have and then, in effect, have your résumé printed in one of the more widely read sections of the Sunday paper.

10

Registries, Wedding Showers, and Thank-You Notes

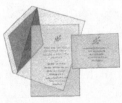

A wedding registry is a different beast from a wish list given to your parents before your birthday or letters written to Santa Claus. First of all, when you wrote those lists or addressed an envelope to the North Pole, you were probably five years old and had no qualms about telling people what you wanted. An endless barrage of commercials during Saturday-morning cartoons told you that getting the latest toys was your divine right as a child.

But now that you and your fiancée are adults, you might find the very idea of a gift registry—essentially a sometimes intricately detailed list of gifts you want from your guests—a little tacky. It's one thing to tell your mommy you want a lollipop or cookie when she took you on errands as a child and carried you as she stood in line at the bank, but it's another to tell your guests you want a digital candy thermometer and an insulated cookie sheet when you're an investment banker.

Don't worry. Wedding registries are as common a part of getting married as champagne and cake. Sure, you can get away with not registering, especially if you and your fiancée are older and already have a complete set of dishes or a nice set of silver that you inherited from a grandparent. But even if you think you have everything you need, there will always be people who want to buy you and your fiancée *something*.

A registry takes the guesswork out of gift giving, which for even the most tasteful and thoughtful guest can be difficult. With friends and family scattered across the country or around the globe, you'll undoubtedly invite plenty of relatives who may have known you well as a towheaded moppet or pimply teenager, but who haven't seen you in years. If your aunts, uncles, and parents' friends have never set foot in your apartment, how will they know that your taste is more retro than preppy, more downtown hipster than suburban country club?

Registering is, of course, a huge convenience for you and your fiancée as well. It not only helps you avoid being stuck with dozens of presents you will never use or even want to see on display in your home, but it can also prevent you from receiving three blenders, twenty salad tongs, and other duplicate gifts that will only have to be returned.

Gift registries come with a specific etiquette meant to make sure the focus stays on your relationship and off the more material aspects of your wedding. But like any Engaged Groom, you already knew that. Even if you like cooking and the thought of getting a new set of stainless steel pots makes you salivate more than Pavlov's dogs, you should never treat your registry as a free-for-all or a loot grab meant to yield you and your bride the highest return on your investment in your wedding.

The traditional view of wedding registries is that the gifts a couple selects should be things that will help them start their new life together as they build a matrimonial home. Friends and family are always happy to help a green-faced young couple, fresh from college or just starting out in their professional careers, stock cabinets and decorate a home that they will share for decades to come. People also like to give gifts knowing that both the bride and the groom will be able to use and enjoy them. For that reason, commonly used housewares such as dishes, pots and pans, and bed linens dominate most gift registries. Department stores, kitchen-supply shops, home-furnishing chains, and catchall superstores are common places where many brides and grooms register.

Not that you should see your wedding as a treasure hunt, but if you invite two hundred people to your wedding and they spend an average of $100 per gift, you and your bride might receive over $20,000 worth of presents. Multiply that by the millions of people getting married each year and you'll understand why all types of stores beyond the big retail players want a piece of the action. For that reason, many stores have special employees whose job it is to help engaged couples put registries together. These "registry consultants" will give you sample lists and point you to popular items that you may not have considered. While 99 percent of these people are especially helpful and polite, remember that 100 percent of them work for the stores at which you register. A good salesperson will guide your hand rather than squeeze it, but having an idea of what you need and want before you start selecting items can help keep you from being pressured into registering for items that are so expensive none of your guests can afford to buy them.

In addition to being a good defense against pushy sales-people, taking stock of what you already have at home and what you are likely to use in the future is a good idea for a more practical reason. Think about the life you will lead and where you will lead it once you are married. If you and your fiancée are teetotaling vegetarians from Arizona, you'll have little use for martini glasses, steak knives, and a down com-forter.

When choosing stores at which to register, don't let the shiny coffeepots and silverware cloud your vision. Consider your guests. You and your bride might want to register at high-end stores such as Tiffany, but not all of your guests will have Bill Gates–sized fortunes with which to buy you a present. Spreading your registry out to three or four differ-ent stores—everything from a high-end department store to more common mall stores such as Crate & Barrel—will give your guests different options. Target and Bed Bath & Be-yond and other big stores often have the same items as their department store counterparts at prices that are a little easier on your guests' pocketbooks. For every expensive appliance or china place setting, add a few items to your registry that your more budget-conscious guests will be able to buy, such as kitchen gadgets, inexpensive picture frames, and basics like place mats or oven mitts.

No matter how much you register for and what you choose, some guests will still want to go off registry when buying you a present, searching for something a tad more meaningful than waffle irons and pillowcases. Remember that a registry is merely a guide for your guests and by no means should anyone be instructed to stick to the list or else. You may wind up with some ugly vases as a result, but not always. My sister, who felt that her close relation warranted a more meaningful gift than a couple of pillowcases, bought us a bottle of wine and a gift certificate to the restaurant where Leora and I had dinner on the night of our engagement.

CLIP 'N' SAVE—A SAMPLE GIFT REGISTRY

The list on the next pages assumes you are starting from scratch. Most people will set a table for eight to twelve people when they host dinners, but if larger family gatherings are in your future, you will want to adjust quantities—more formal dinnerware and wineglasses, for example—accordingly. Also, adjust or eliminate other categories depending on your needs.

For the uninitiated, a dinnerware place setting usually includes a dinner plate, salad plate, soup or cereal bowl, and a mug. Some formal dinnerware might also include a bread or dessert plate. Silver and flatware sets include a salad fork, dinner fork, knife, soupspoon, and teaspoon. With glassware, order the same amount as your dinnerware. Although many couples order one set of formal dinnerware and another set for everyday use, one way to save money or cut down on the size of your registry is to order two sets of dishes, but only one set of silverware to match both. Depending on how much you drink, you might also find a set of wineglasses that can be used for formal get-togethers and casual after-work drinks.

As for bedding, you'll probably want at least three to four sets of sheets. Pillows and comforters can be limited to as many as you would use at one time on a bed. In the bathroom, shoot for six to eight of each item to account for the frequency with which you and your possible guests use towels.

Formal Dinnerware

__ place settings

__ dessert plates

__ soup bowls

__ creamer & sugar bowl

__ gravy boat

__ salt/pepper shakers

__ serving bowls

__ covered serving dishes

__ serving platters

Formal Silver

__ place settings

__ serving pieces

__ butter knives

Everyday Dinnerware

__ place settings

__ creamer & sugar bowl

__ salt/pepper shakers

__ serving bowls

__ covered serving dishes

__ serving platters

Everyday Flatware

__ place settings

__ serving pieces

Drinkware

__ tall drink glasses

__ double old-fashioned glasses

__ red & white wineglasses

__ champagne flutes

Barware

__ highball glasses

__ brandy glasses

__ martini glasses

__ pilsner glasses

Cookware

__ saucepans

__ sauté pans

__ stockpot

__ steamer/double boiler

__ teakettle

__ wok/stir-fry pan

Cookware
__ lasagna pan

__ casserole dishes

__ roasting pan

__ grill pan

__ pancake griddle

__ omelet pan

Bakeware
__ cookie sheets

__ muffin pans

__ cake & pie pans

__ loaf pan

Kitchen Tools
__ measuring cups/
spoons

__ mixing bowls

__ cooking/serving utensils

__ dish towels/oven mitts

__ storage containers

__ miscellaneous gadgets

Appliances
__ mixer

__ toaster

__ food processor

__ blender

__ coffeemaker

__ waffle iron

__ hand mixer

__ indoor grill

__ ice cream maker

Cutlery
(The first four items often come as part of a block set.)

__ paring knife

__ chef knife

__ bread knife

__ carving knife

__ 8–12 steak knives

Bedding
__ pillowcases

__ pillow shams

__ fitted sheets

__ flat sheets

__ comforter

__ blankets

__ pillows

Bathroom Stuff
__ bath sheets
(large towels)

__ towels

__ hand towels

__ washcloths

__ bath rug

__ shower curtain/liner

__ shower curtain rings

Miscellaneous

__ vases

__ picture frames

__ bowls

__ candlesticks

__ lamps

__ tablecloths

__ place mats

__ napkins/napkin rings

A REGISTRY STAPLE—LUGGAGE

Up until now, the only type of baggage you may have thought about is of the emotional nature. But luggage, of the suitcase or folding-suit-bag variety, is a great thing to put on your registry. In fact, luggage sets have long been popular engagement or shower presents, as many people like to give them to couples in advance of the honeymoon. Unless you're planning to take a blender on your honeymoon, your luggage will be one of the first wedding presents you use, which is an idea that sits well with guests. A typical luggage set, which includes rolling suitcases, garment bags, one larger suitcase, and carry-on bags can typically be found at the same store where you selected many of your other gifts, but don't think that expensive department-store prices are your only option. Specialty retailers such as L.L. Bean and REI carry cheaper and oftentimes more durable bags than do general-purpose department stores.

THE THRILL OF THE BUNDT—WHAT TO BRING WITH YOU WHEN YOU REGISTER

Registering is a lot like hunting except that instead of finding wild game in the jungles of South America or on safari in Africa, you'll set out through canyons of coffeepots and jungles of bedsheets and bath towels in the aisles of Macy's or Marshall Field's. Picking off items with your electronic scanning gun, you'll add things to your registry with the skill of a master marksman tracking down his prey. The frying pans are on the fifth floor? No problem. You love the smell of stainless steel in the morning.

Like any good hunter, it will help to have the right equipment and attitude when you go on your excursion. Department stores are hot, noisy, and crowded places, and tensions can easily run high when you're arguing with your bride over china patterns and whether you need an espresso maker that says the time out loud. Don't get too hung up on exactly what you need, and if you and your fiancée wind up disagreeing about something, it doesn't hurt to add it now and think about it later. In fact, once you've selected a number of gifts, your registry will most likely be available for you to check out online so you can add and remove items from home. Bring a bottle of water so you don't wind up lost in the lingerie department searching for a water fountain. A digital camera is a good way to settle any argument; if you aren't sure if something will match the walls in your apartment or your bedroom furniture, snap a picture and check it when you get home. Build in a lunch break by making reservations at a nearby restaurant or by vowing to stop what you are doing and heading over to the food court midway through your day.

Things You Might Want to Register For, but Shouldn't

There's no rule that says you have to stick to the traditional wedding registry of soupspoons and tablecloths if you and your fiancée already have a fully stocked kitchen. I'll cover alternatives to the traditional registry in the next section, but beware. It's considered poor form to put any of the following on your list.

- **CDs, DVDs, and books.** Getting married is not a chance to get that boxed set you always wanted or to build your library. Greatest-hits collections, special-edition DVDs, or the latest Hollywood blockbuster are big no-no's. The only books that should make it onto your registry are cookbooks, which are typically available from the store where you will register for kitchenware.
- **Clothes.** Wedding gifts are meant to last a lifetime, not a season.
- **Computer and electronic equipment.** A flat-screen TV and a new laptop might be things you use in your home, but they don't exactly qualify as

household items. Most consumer electronics will be obsolete before your first wedding anniversary anyway, and people like to come to your home and see their gifts getting good use many years into your marriage. However, digital cameras—which can be used to take pictures on your honeymoon—are increasingly becoming an exception to this rule.

- **Food.** Friends might throw in a bottle of extravirgin olive oil with the gift of a frying pan or some organic pancake mix with a high-end griddle, but registering for edible items is a big no-no. A useful key: the expiration date on the gifts you pick should be later than your fifth anniversary.

BEYOND BED AND BATH—
GETTING CREATIVE WITH YOUR REGISTRY

So, knowing that the new U2 album and a complete set of *Star Trek* DVDs are not exactly the most acceptable of wedding presents, what can you do if you already have a high-tech cof-feemaker, comfy bed linens, and other staples of a traditional wedding registry? In recent years it has become acceptable for couples to expand their registries to include gifts reflecting their hobbies, passions, and needs beyond cooking big meals. Here's a sampling of some things you might choose to ask for:

- **Camping equipment.** If you and your bride share a passion for the outdoors, your guests will probably be happy to buy you a tent, cookout gear, and other Grizzly Adams–type supplies. Don't be too specific with the gear requests, and remember what I said about clothing: a two-person pup tent is fine, but a pair of size ten hiking boots is not.

- **Home improvement tools.** They might not be the most romantic of gifts, but shovels and lawn trimmers can be as useful in your new home as spatulas and egg whisks. The Home Depot and other big hardware stores have gotten in on the registry act, knowing that couples are thinking outside of the kitchen.

- **Honeymoons.** Many Web sites allow you to register for "pieces" of your honeymoon: a night in a hotel, dinner for two, airfare, etc. Having guests pay for your big vacation is a relatively new practice, so don't be surprised if the idea confuses or even offends some more traditional friends and family. Also, writing thank-you notes for such gifts presents an interesting challenge. "Dear Uncle Jim and Aunt Irene, thank you for the gift of one night's stay at the charming bed-and-breakfast. Leora and I thought of you as we spent our first night together as husband and wife."

- **Charitable donations.** Truly the perfect gift for the couple that has everything. Some couples alert their guests that in lieu of gifts, donations can be made to a specific charity with special meaning to the bride and groom. Be aware that some guests

might still feel the need to buy you a present or
donate to a charity you did not specify, especially
if they don't share your political or social values.

A DIFFERENT KIND OF CASH REGISTER—
ASKING FOR MONEY

Like many couples just starting out, you and your fiancée
might need a bigger nest egg more than a new egg whisk.
Even if you are older and more settled, you may find that
the years you've spent on your own have given you plenty of
time to amass a kitchenful of nice appliances and a bedroom
with perfectly comfortable sheets and pillows, and that what
you really need now is a house in which to plant some roots.
If what you really need is money, do you still have to register for physical presents?

As is the theme elsewhere in this book, the answer, of
course, is that you don't *have* to do anything. Asking for
cash has become an increasingly popular alternative to standard wedding registries and, in fact, is part and parcel of
some cultural traditions. But on a wider scale, asking solely
for cash is still largely uncharted territory and should be ap-
proached carefully with due respect for etiquette and the
message you wish to send.

If you are asking for cash, it's always a good idea to first
ask why you need it before telling friends and family that's
what you want. If your goal is to save for a down payment
on your first home, I say go for it. As I mentioned before, the
idea of wedding presents has largely been to help couples be-

gin their new life together. Helping you purchase a home in which to start your marriage certainly jives with that idea. Writing checks to help you buy a new luxury car does not.

Money, whether it's the $200 you're hoping to get from your aunt Harriet for your wedding or the twenty bucks a friend owes you for his bar tab, is never an easy subject. Because of the pressure put on couples to register for housewares, asking for cash is not something that might sit well with you, even if it's what you really need. But as I've already warned you, never include gift information on your invitations. That warning should go double if you are planning to ask for cash.

So how do you get the word out? The best way is to tell your parents your intentions. When relatives call them to ask what they can get you, your mother or father or your bride's parents can politely tell them, for example, "What Doug and Leora really want to do is buy a house this year. They'd appreciate money more than anything." No one should be told *not* to buy you physical gifts, but once the information is out there that you'd rather have cash, your guests will make up their own minds. You'll still probably wind up with some vases and picture frames, but most people will be happy to save themselves a trip to the mall by writing you a check.

If you do ask for cash, you might turn to the Internet and one of the many Web sites that allow couples to register for cash and even stock and securities. A couple in the midst of planning a wedding created one popular site, and their intentions were innocent enough. While registering for housewares, the couple realized that people often have greater needs than just glassware and bedsheets. With no acceptable way to ask for cash, they decided to create their dot-com baby: an online gift registry that would allow en-gaged couples and other people in their financial infancy to start off on the right foot.

So they didn't feel comfortable asking people for cash, but they did feel comfortable asking people to visit a Web site for the sole purpose of giving cash? How did that make it easier? Nevertheless, such e-businesses are taking off, billing themselves as "quick and easy" ways for guests to give new couples a much-needed infusion of cold, hard cash.

The above-mentioned Web site charges gift givers trans-action fees ranging from $5 for gifts of $100 to 4 percent for gifts over $500. I fail to see how paying $24 to give someone $600 is any easier than writing a check, putting it in a card, and handing an envelope to the recipient. Even if a guest wanted to mail you a check, we're still a long way away from the time when postage rates would approach the "conve-nience" fees of these online opportunists. Avoid online cash registries like day-old shrimp cocktail at a buffet.

CASH AND CARRY— RETURNING GIFTS FOR CASH

If you want to ask for cash but are nervous about it, don't let anyone tell you that you can just return all your gifts and get a pile of cash in exchange. First of all, this practice will send you into prickly ethical territory, and from a more practical perspective, many stores simply don't allow it.

If people see a gift on your registry and buy it for you, they are doing so because they think you want it and will use it. It would be one thing to return a gift because you have already received the same thing from someone else, but it's another thing altogether to explain to someone that you had no intention of using his present to begin with. He'll likely feel hurt or offended, feelings he might not have had had you simply asked for cash in the first place.

It might be hard to feel sorry for corporate behemoths such as department stores or mall chain stores, but there's an ethical implication to consider there as well. Loading up your registry with products at a store that specializes in wedding registries if you're only intending to return everything once the wedding is over is a waste of everyone's time and not the reason these stores are in business. In fact, because so many couples have taken advantage of historically generous return policies at places that specialize in wedding registries, many stores no longer give cash for gift returns and will instead issue store credit only.

SHOWER THE PEOPLE—
AN ENGAGED GROOM'S LOOK
AT WEDDING SHOWERS

Sometime before your wedding, someone will throw a shower in honor of your fiancée. While traditionally organized by the maid of honor or friends of the bride's family and attended only by women, the times are indeed a-changin'. Today it is not unheard of for the groom to make more than just a token pop-in appearance, and the parties themselves are increasingly becoming a coed affair.

A wedding shower can take many forms—a brunch, afternoon luncheon, or informal dinner—but most will involve the guest or guests of honor opening presents in front of the assembled guests, a situation that for an Engaged Groom and his bride is understandably uncomfortable. Sure, plenty of people are used to opening gifts in front of large groups of people, but they are either young children tearing open boxes of LEGO toys at birthday parties or retirees receiving a gold watch at a corporate dinner.

If you've registered, opening your gifts in front of the people who bought them for you presents a unique challenge. It's not that you aren't grateful for your presents and the expense and effort involved in getting them for you, but how do you show your appreciation and feign surprise when (a) you know what you are getting and (b) you know how much everything cost? "Wow! The electric mixer we picked out for ourselves! Thanks, Uncle Kenny! Now we know your love for us is worth $39.99 plus tax!"

While some shower organizers and other traditionalists will insist on having you and your bride open presents in front of everyone, you and your bride might politely ask that the focus of the party be on eating, drinking, and socializing with friends and family, not oohing and aahing over shiny cookie sheets, juice glasses, and butter dishes.

ENGAGED GROOM TIP

Can You Use the Gifts before the Wedding?

When it comes to gifts, some couples follow tradition to the letter, having everything sent to the bride's parents' home and waiting to use everything until after the wedding. But if you were such a traditionalist—and as an Engaged Groom, you probably are not—the plain fact is that you and your fiancée wouldn't be living together, as most couples do these days before getting married. Today, it seems as if the only benefit to having gifts sent to your in-laws-to-be is the extra storage space and having someone to sign for the packages.

The short answer to the use-or-don't-use argument is that people buy gifts because they want the recipients to enjoy using them. If you have an engagement party at which gifts are given, those presents can reasonably be considered engagement gifts, and therefore it is acceptable to use them whether or not the people who gave them to you plan on giving you another present for your wedding. Anyone who doesn't want you to use gifts before you are married will wait to give you a present until your wedding day or sometime shortly after.

THE RIGHT ATTITUDE
FOR GRATITUDE—THANK-YOU NOTES

For an Engaged Groom, there is perhaps nothing more important than expressing your gratitude to friends, family, and other invited guests in a timely manner for the generous gifts they will give you simply because you are getting married. The proper way to do that, of course, is with a handwritten thank-you note. In our electronic age, such notes are going the way of the dodo bird, surviving only for weddings and more formal occasions. Therefore, you and your bride may be a tad out of practice when it comes to giving thanks to people on paper.

Plan to get personalized stationery to use as thank-you notes. Stationery stores and any place that prints wedding invitations will have samples of designs from which you can choose. For easy, one-stop shopping, have your thank-you notes made at the same time as your invitations and see if the printer will give you a break on the price in exchange for you giving him or her more of your business.

The more computer-savvy you are, the more comfortable you may be designing your own thank-you notes and having them printed at your local copy shop, saving you perhaps hundreds of dollars. No matter what method you choose, thank-you notes should reflect that your guests have spent a considerable amount of money and effort in selecting, buying, and, in most cases, shipping gifts to you and your fiancée. Therefore, picking up a pack of twenty note cards for a few bucks at your corner drugstore is probably not a good idea.

TIMING IS EVERYTHING—
WHEN DO THEY GO OUT?

Gifts received before the wedding should be followed up with a thank-you note within two to three weeks. Because gifts will trickle in before your wedding, it's best to stay on top of this before the deluge that inevitably happens immediately after the big day. Thank-you notes for gifts received at or immediately following your wedding should be sent within four to five weeks.

ENGAGED GROOM TIP

I'll Do Yours If You'll Do Mine

Split the thank-you-note writing duties fifty-fifty with your fiancée and suggest that you write all the notes to her friends and family and she write all the notes to yours. When your fiancée's aunt and uncle receive a note from the new nephew-in-law—if such a term exists—they'll appreciate your gratitude that much more and will feel as if they are getting to know the new addition to their extended family. If you are a little shy about such things, you can still split the job fifty-fifty, but with each of you sticking to your own friends and family. (It should go without saying, but both you and your bride should sign each note, no matter who wrote it.)

I'M NOT A POET AND I DEFINITELY KNOW IT—WHAT DO I WRITE?

You face a number of challenges in expressing your appreciation for presents, especially when those presents may not be too dissimilar from each other. These challenges will become clearer to you with each successive note you write. The first ten might be easy enough, but how do you make hundreds of letters convey your true gratitude for your guests' thoughtfulness? After a while, it can be hard not to feel as if you are playing a giant game of Mad Libs.

Dear (PERSON'S NAME),

Thank you for the (NOUN). It was so (ADJECTIVE) and we look forward to using it for (ACTIVITY) as we (VERB) our new life together. We hope to see you in (PLACE) for (EVENT) soon.

Love,
(BRIDE AND GROOM)

Making each note personal can be a challenge, but one trick is to tie the gift to something specific you plan to do with it. For example:

- "Leora can't wait to make pies this Thanksgiving in the beautiful pie plate. We'll save you a slice!"

- "We're looking forward to offering many toasts in
  the champagne flutes you gave us and will be sure
  to raise a glass in your honor soon."

If you are writing a note to thank someone for a gift of
cash, never mention the exact amount. Instead refer to it
as a "generous gift" and perhaps mention your plans for
the money: "Thank you for your generous gift. Leora and
I are planning to buy a house next year, and we appreciate
the support of our family in helping us reach that goal."
(If you do wind up buying a house with some of the
money you received from your friends and family, follow
up with them later by sending a picture of the house and
another note of thanks when the deal is sealed and you are
moved in.)

Personalizing your response to every gift might not be
possible, of course. After all, how many things can you say
about a spatula? One solution is to focus on people's efforts
to attend your wedding and how much you appreciated their
presence: "That you flew all the way from Iceland is an incredible honor, and we were so happy that we had the
chance to celebrate with you." If you're planning to see
someone soon at an occasion unrelated to your wedding,
you might mention how much you are looking forward to
that event.

Being courteous has its practical advantages as well.
Writing a thank-you note can alert your guests to any mix-
ups that may have occurred between their ordering your gift
and your receiving it. If a store forgot to put two dishes in a
box and sent only one, a well-written thank-you note will let
them know that something didn't get sent and they'll be able

to fix the problem. One groom who wrote to some friends thanking them for a picture frame later received a phone call from them wondering why he hadn't mentioned the check included in the box. He hadn't mentioned it because he hadn't noticed the envelope buried beneath a mound of crumpled tissue paper.

MAKING A LIST, CHECKING IT TWICE— KEEPING TRACK OF GIFTS AND THANK-YOU NOTES

Even if you are having a relatively small wedding of less than one hundred people, you can still expect to receive dozens of presents. Without some system for keeping track of them all, you will soon forget who sent what and whether you sent a thank-you note for each specific gift.

Using the guest database or spreadsheet you created earlier, copy your guest list and paste it to a new sheet. (You can also just add additional columns to your master guest list if that's easier for you.) Create two columns. Label one with the heading "Gift," and underneath type in the name or short description of each gift you received from the corresponding guest on the left. Next to that column, under the heading "Note Sent," type the date when you mailed the thank-you note.

Keeping this list updated will prevent a moment of panic ten minutes before your cousins Barbara and Richard come over if you can't remember whether you sent them a thank-you note for the plates on which you're about to serve dinner.

GIFTS/THANK-YOU NOTES

LAST NAME	FIRST NAME
Anderson	Nicholas and Marita
Bennett	Leigh and Scott
Birnbaum	Amy and Adam
Boxt	Jason and Rosalie
Cunningham	Lew, Moira, Zach, and Zoe
Gordon	Kenneth, Dara, Michael, and Laura
Gordon	Miriam
Hirschfield	Irene and James
Hirschfield	Jordan and Jody
Lerner	Sidney and Blossom
Mates-Muchin	JT and Jacqueline
Perry	James
Rigler	Peter and Stacey
Silverman	Alan and Michelle

THROWING IT ALL AWAY—GETTING RID OF UNWANTED GIFTS

Even with the great care that has gone into creating your registry and the great care with which your guests selected gifts, every bride and groom gets stuck with some things

GIFT	NOTE SENT
ice cream maker	9-Mar
gravy boat	13-May
red flower vase	21-Feb
$100 check	17-Jan
pancake griddle	15-Jul
6 white wine glasses	7-Jul
$250 check	15-Aug
food processor	7-Aug
$75 check	26-Jul
2 sets everyday flatware	3-Jun
4 champagne flutes	16-Aug
casserole dish and oven mitts	28-Mar
espresso maker	17-May
2 cookie sheets and 2 pie tins	13-Aug

they simply don't want. If only getting rid of that ugly ceramic bowl or the pastel salad tongs was as simple as handing them to a stranger on the street. While that may be an option—albeit one that makes people wonder about the crazy couple handing out kitchen supplies on the street—remember that if it's the thought that counts when someone buys you a gift, be sure to give a lot of thought when getting rid of one. Your options include:

- **Regifting.** If you didn't want it, why would anyone else? Only use this option if you have to get a present for someone you don't like much. Friends don't give friends ugly picture frames.
- **Charity.** The best option for the socially conscious couple. Beware, however. Just because people are poor doesn't mean they have bad taste.
- **Garage sale.** Warning! Do not attempt if the person who gave you the present lives in your neighborhood. Talk about awkward.
- **eBay.** Anonymous, safe, and secure, online auctions might be your best option. There is only a 1 in 12,649,852 chance you'll sell it back to the person who got it for you.

Remember that you may have to hold on to some gifts, no matter how tacky they are. When your cousin Leigh and her husband, Scott, come over for dinner, they may wonder why you're not pouring drinks out of that Mount Saint Helens–shaped pitcher they bought you as an engagement present.

ENGAGED GROOM TIP

Stop the Wedding Gift Insanity!

If you are especially close with a tight circle of friends, it might seem silly to buy presents for them only to have them spend the same amount on you later, especially if you are only one of many people in your crew getting married in the coming months and years. My friends, all in their late twenties and early thirties, go to an average of four or five weddings per year and buy a present for each couple. It can be expensive, especially when one considers the larger costs associated with attending a wedding. As a result, my friends instituted a One Wedding, One Gift pact. Rather than worry about buying an engagement present, shower gift, and another for the wedding itself, my friends and I have vowed to limit our gifts to one per couple. This stops the endless flow of gifts back and forth between friends and helps us all keep costs down so we can focus on more important things, like having a good time.

If your groomsmen and your fiancée's bridesmaids are taking an active role in the wedding, you may want to consider letting them off the hook when it comes to gifts. After a weekend bachelor party in Las Vegas during which my groomsmen and close friends dropped a large chunk of change on airfare, hotels, meals, gambling, and miscellaneous expenses, I decided they had spent more than enough money and told them not to buy me and Leora a present. (I discussed this with her before making this announcement to my friends, of course.) After all, on my twenty-fifth wedding anniversary, what will I remember more? The good time I had with my friends or that one of them bought me an asparagus steamer?

Leora took a similar approach with her bridesmaids, telling them that the money they spent on their dresses was present enough. Although some people wound up buying us gifts anyway, no one felt obligated, and we more or less avoided hearing any complaints about the amount of money it cost our friends just to show up at our wedding.

Stopping the wedding gift insanity and the sheer volume of material stuff that flows back and forth between friends is a great way to keep the focus of your wedding where it belongs: on the love between you and your bride and the fact that you want to share a happy time with your close friends and family.

Part Three

TAKING A BREAK . . .
SORT OF

After the initial burst of planning and possibly months of meetings, food tastings, and other big decisions, you and your bride may experience a quiet before the storm. So much gets done so quickly that many couples get to a midpoint in their wedding planning and find that, for at least a little while, there isn't a whole lot to do. I'm sure you and your bride have a veritable laundry list of tasks waiting to be accomplished, but many of them—confirming final numbers with a caterer, applying for a marriage license, making a seating chart for your reception—can't be done until the final month or so before your wedding.

This middle period is a real luxury. It affords you the opportunity to focus on some of the more fun aspects of wedding planning. You might start thinking about the rehearsal dinner, a celebration that's typically a little looser in form and style than a wedding reception. You and your bride are probably taking a honeymoon after your wedding, and now is a great time to work out some of the more specific details beyond when and where you want to go.

Now that the big tasks have been taken care of and you're just waiting for your wedding date to come around, you might use this time to catch up on a few things. If you've received so many gifts that you're on a first-name basis with your UPS guy—mine is named Kenny and probably knows what Leora and I received for our wedding better than we do—write a few thank-you notes before you get too far behind. Double-check your budget to see if any vendors are still awaiting payments, and make sure you haven't maxed out any categories. Chat with your bandleader to make sure he has a copy of the song you want him to play for your first dance. Meet with your priest, rabbi, or other officiant.

Most important, don't forget your date night. Your wedding might not change much about your relationship besides its legal status, but the dates you go on as two people who are about to be married will probably feel different from the dates you go on as newlyweds. Make the most of these regular check-ins with your fiancée, and you'll be ready for the whirlwind that will inevitably begin once this middle period is over.

11

The Rehearsal Dinner, Favors, and Other Guest Issues

Making sure your guests are entertained and know where to be when can take a lot of effort and coordination. This is a chance for the real Engaged Groom to show his talents, as many of the things that have served you well at work or in your personal life—your organizational skills, your reputation for throwing a good party—can come into focus during this period of the wedding planning. Even in the most traditional of weddings, a groom and his family will be involved with much of what happens from here on out. The rehearsal dinner, of course, is just one area that may be your territory.

ALL TOGETHER NOW—IT'S NOT CALLED A REHEARSAL DINNER FOR NOTHING

Some couples and families are so focused on partying and impressing their guests they forget that a rehearsal dinner is supposed to follow an actual run-through of your wedding ceremony. Talk with your priest, rabbi, or other officiant about scheduling a rehearsal for the day before your wedding, so that every participant knows what to do during your ceremony. If at all possible, hold the rehearsal in the same place where you are planning to get married, but if the church is being used for mass or the country club is booked with another event, you might have to be creative. Even if you can't do it on-site, having an informal dress rehearsal will take some of the mystery out of your wedding ceremony, which is always a recipe for soothing even the most nervous of participants. Some of your groomsmen and family members may be participating in a wedding for their first time, so don't skip the practice.

ASSEMBLING THE MASSES— THE REHEARSAL DINNER

Because of the growing pressure in society for couples to have bigger and better weddings than those who went before them, the rehearsal dinner has taken on huge significance. In fact, some people treat them as mini wedding receptions, spending as much on dinner for their guests the night before ling. At destination weddings, this can be expensive, as more likely than not, *all* of the guests will be from out of town. Still, it's the polite thing to do. Just be careful about such a large event. It can turn your rehearsal dinner into *Wedding, Part One*, which is something I've already talked about trying to avoid.

One way to avoid this, of course, is to have the rehearsal dinner in a space as different from your wedding reception venue as possible. Many restaurants have space for large groups, and a family member might have enough backyard space for a more casual type of party. If you want to give your guests an authentic experience, why not try sampling some of the local cuisine? A pasta dinner in Little Italy, a Chinese buffet in Chinatown, a Texas barbecue, or a clambake on a beach in Maine can be a lot more fun and festive than a sit-down dinner in a generic restaurant. Not that your guests won't already be excited to share your wedding with you and your bride, but they'll definitely appreciate an experience they don't normally get at home.

Aside from eating—and, yes, there will be a lot of eating—what happens at a rehearsal dinner? The answer can be anything from "not much" to "a heck of a lot." If you are having a small dinner with only immediate family and wedding party members, you and your bride might use the event as an opportunity to thank them for their participation and present them with thank-you gifts. Since toasting at a wedding is typically left to parents, siblings, and your best man, some guests might use the rehearsal dinner as an opportunity to raise their glass in your honor with a few kind words or funny stories. At our rehearsal dinner,

the wedding as they will for lunch at the rece
day. While I would not recommend that your
ner be an elaborate event—you want to save s
for the actual wedding, after all—you can still
of fun. It's a chance for even the least Engag
take the reins and have a good time.

Traditionally, a groom's parents plan and
hearsal dinner. It's not necessarily a small expens
parents don't have a lot of experience with w
honest with them about what is expected, even i
getting too involved with the planning. As the
in your immediate family who is likely to know
tant players in your bride's, you'll be an invalua
coordinating any type of prewedding rehearsal ev

Whom should you invite to your rehearsal di
bare minimum, anyone who is participating in y
ding should be there: immediate family, grooms
bridesmaids. Those people also get to bring wi
bands, dates, or anyone else who is accompanying
your wedding, so don't make their significant other
the hotel while the wedding party chows down. It sl
without saying, but an invitation should also be ext
whoever is performing your wedding. A rabbi or pr
forms weddings as a regular part of his job, and just
want to get a good night's rest before a big present
work, the person officiating at your wedding might n
to be out late the night before, eating and drinking
though you'll send him an invitation, don't expect you
ciant to come.

It's customary to invite all out-of-town guests inst
making them fend for themselves the night before your

some of our friends prepared slide shows with embarrassing childhood photos, while others gave us the kind of good-natured roasting that might not have been inappropriate in a more formal setting.

How do you get the word out about your rehearsal dinner? You can include extra information with formal wedding invitations, but make sure you have a good system of keeping track, or you'll wind up inviting everyone to an event that was meant for out-of-town guests only. Some couples wait until response cards start coming in to send out invitations to other events over the wedding weekend. I would not recommend waiting that long, as you might risk complicating the already-booked travel plans of good friends and family. If you are mailing separate rehearsal dinner invitations, do it within one week of mailing your regular invitations.

ASK NOT WHAT YOUR GUESTS CAN DO FOR YOU—FAVORS AND OTHER TOKENS OF APPRECIATION

Seeing as how your guests are traveling to your wedding and giving up a prime Saturday night to party with you and your families, the least you could do is show them how much you appreciate the effort. For that reason, many couples purchase small favors to give to their guests at one of two places: the reception site or hotel.

At the reception, favors such as candles or bags of fancy candy are placed at each seat for guests to take home. Some couples combine the place card with the favor, using small picture frames to hold cards on which a guest's name and table number is written. Offering your guests favors at your reception is by no means a requirement and, with two hundred people and a few dollars or more per favor, can be quite expensive. (Some people see their feeding guests as enough of an expense and thus do not leave favors at the tables.)

Even if you don't give your guests favors at the wedding reception, you should prepare something for those friends and family members staying at local hotels so they are not held hostage to their room's minibar. But don't think you have to break the bank here, either. Fill a small gift bag with bottles of water, a pack of gum or mints, chocolates, snacks, and other goodies. You might also include a note welcoming people to the hotel and a schedule of the weekend's events. Brochures or information on local points of interest might help your guests fill the downtime between wedding-related events. Call local tourist attractions and see if you can't negotiate a special discount for your guests at area attractions and include tickets or coupons along with everything else you've assembled. The hotel's registration desk can present these gift bags at check-in or place them in each room in advance of your guests' arrival. (Any hotel that is used to blocking rooms for big events such as weddings should be able to accommodate you, but speak with a manager before dropping off hundreds of gift bags at the bell desk.)

ENGAGED GROOM TIP

Does Anyone Really Need This Junk?

Scented candles made with the essence of your fiancée's favorite flowers. Candy tins etched with your names and the date of your wedding. Bottles of water personalized with labels featuring your names and wedding date. Chocolate bars with your initials molded right in. If your bride has spent any time online recently or if you've flipped through any wedding magazines or catalogs, you may have noticed an incredible amount of things available for personalization. One wedding Web site even offers personalized confetti. Yes, you read that right: pieces of confetti so small you'd need a microscope to really make out the bride's and groom's names printed on each tiny shred.

When you decide what to give your guests, don't get suckered in by wedding Web sites offering specially designed, wedding-themed favors. You can usually find the same things at party supply stores and gift wholesalers for much less. Remember that the word *wedding*, when it appears before any good or service—wedding candle, wedding flowers, wedding cake, wedding fortune cookies—just means that you'll pay more for something you can get just about anywhere.

You can treat your guests to something more specific by giving them something that reflects the local culture. A bottle of Vermont maple syrup or Texas barbecue sauce might be more interesting than a tin of mints or a scented candle.

As much as your guests might appreciate the favors, they won't probably care if they go home without one. In fact, your guests might forget to bring them home anyway, no matter what you give them. Ask any caterers about cleaning up after a wedding and they'll tell you that they often pick up lots of unclaimed favors. Taking home favors from a wedding is probably not the highest priority for most wedding guests, and that's not surprising. If you had come to my wedding, you wouldn't probably have had much use for a picture frame etched with "Doug & Leora, August 29" on August 30.

Rather than spending hundreds or even thousands of dollars on straight-to-eBay favors, why not consider making a donation to charity in honor of your guests instead? You can have small cards describing the charity printed and left at each table. Pick your charity wisely, of course, as the sheer number of your guests will make it unlikely that everyone follows the same political ideology. Chosen carefully, charitable donations are the perfect wedding favor. If your guests decide to take that home, it will do a lot more good for the world than a personalized tin of potpourri.

12

Planning the Honeymoon

Traditionally, making the arrangements for the honeymoon is the groom's domain. So is footing the bill. But like all aspects of the wedding planning, choosing where to go and what to do on your honeymoon is not something that should be left solely up to you. Since your honeymoon will likely be the first thing you and your fiancée do together after you are married, working together on where you take a vacation is a good way to get your marriage started on the right foot.

The first thing you should do is set a budget for your trip. Many couples see the honeymoon as an afterthought and don't factor it into their overall wedding expenses. But ask yourself a question: If you are pushing the upper limits of your budget just to have your wedding, will you really enjoy your honeymoon when you are worried about the price of every piña colada and souvenir? The last thing you want to worry about when you're on your honeymoon is how you are going to pay for it all, so work that detail out in advance.

Don't leave honeymoon planning until the last minute. Airline fares, hotel rates, and other travel expenses tend to go up during the busy summer months, so act fast if you want a good deal. If you've booked your wedding date far enough in advance, you should have a solid idea of when you want to travel. Such knowledge of your schedule gives you an advantage, as booking months or even a year before you want to travel may entitle you to your choice of seats, rooms, and dinner reservations.

One way to save money is to hold off on leaving until a few days after your wedding. Many couples, married on a Saturday night, head to the airport the next day to start their honeymoon. But Sunday is a notoriously busy day for travel, and flying on a weekend will mean that you'll compete for fares and legroom with all the other weekend travelers.

Waiting a day or two to begin your honeymoon has other benefits as well. You might not want to get up early the day after your wedding to catch a plane—the dread of a 6 a.m. wake-up call can kill a romantic wedding night—and with all the other things you may have to deal with on your wedding day, worrying about packing is not the best way to spend your first few hours together as husband and wife.

Once you've decided when you can go and how much you can spend, obviously you have to decide what type of trip you want to take. If you and your fiancée have both caught the same kind of travel bug, congratulations. You'll have a much easier time planning the honeymoon. But if you tend to like white-water rafting and mountain climbing, and your bride likes strolling through quaint European cities and winery tours, you'll have to find some room for compromise. The easiest solution is to divide the trip in two, spending, say, one week hiking through a jungle and one week visiting museums and soaking in the local culture. You may be able to do both at once, as many resorts offer activities and day trips to cater to adventure enthusiasts and the more laid-back alike.

Of course, relaxing may be just what you need after months or a year or more of hard-core wedding planning, so don't rule out a beach resort or other peaceful option. The week before your wedding can be the most stressful time of your entire engagement, so keep that in mind when you plan your trip. Booking a fifty-mile bike tour for the Monday after your wedding might be more than you can handle after what is bound to be a busy and emotional wedding day.

CARDED—NAME CHANGES AND TRAVEL DOCUMENTS

If your bride is taking your name immediately after the wedding, make sure that the legal documents she will need for travel reflect that change. With airline security as strict as it is, especially for foreign travel, getting on board an airplane when the name on her ticket doesn't match the name on her driver's license or passport can be a major inconvenience for your wife. You wouldn't want to go on your honeymoon alone, would you? Even if you make it to your destination without any problems, if the name on your wife's ID is different from what it says in a hotel computer, getting a replacement for a lost key or charging things to your room might be a hassle. The safest bet is to book all airline tickets and travel arrangements using her maiden name and to wait to make changes to any government-issued documents until after you return from your trip. Talk to a travel agent or someone versed in passport and visa requirements before you head to the airport.

ENGAGED GROOM TIP

Go Away Another Day

Much like the pressure to have a wedding that is bigger and better than everyone else's, many couples feel under the gun to treat their honeymoon as the biggest vacation they'll ever take. And they do it for a reason: getting married is a perfect opportunity to tell your boss you'll be gone for two weeks or more and a good excuse to leave voice mail, e-mail, and other work responsibilities behind. But going away immediately after your wedding for an extended time is not necessarily the best option for everyone. Is it the right one for you?

After missing work for a few days before the wedding to get ready, many couples simply don't have the time they'd like to devote to an extended vacation. Faced with the pressures of busy jobs and demands at home, taking time off on top of the time you might have to take immediately before the wedding could mean sacrificing vacation days on either end of your honeymoon.

Considering the incredible expense of weddings in the first place, many couples these days are opting to delay their honeymoons. The extra time they take before going away can be used to save for an even bigger and better trip. So instead of going away immediately on the trip you think you have to take, waiting to take your honeymoon for a month, six months, or even longer can give you and your fiancée more time to save for the trip you really want to take. Tony, a groom who along with his bride needed a more practical approach to the honeymoon, took a breather before flying the friendly skies. "We waited for our first anniversary before going on a big trip that we called a honeymoon. There just wasn't time right after our wedding, so we put it off, saved money, and did it right."

If you do postpone your honeymoon, take two or three days to go on a quick vacation with your new wife immediately or soon after the wedding anyway, even if it's just to a local bed-and-breakfast or hotel down the street. Taking what I call a minimoon will help you both recharge your batteries as you start your new life together. Above all else, don't go into the office the Monday after your wedding.

13

The Bachelor Party

Don't think that your bachelor party has to be an all-out, hands-down, guys-only, last-blast blowout. In fact, don't think you need to have a bachelor party in the traditional sense or even at all. You're getting married, not heading off to prison, joining the priesthood, or leaving for a ten-year tour of duty. You'll have plenty of chances to party with your friends in the future, and if you're worried that your marriage will mean a loss of your freedom, I suggest you talk to a therapist and not a stripper.

These days, the bachelor party has moved beyond its stag-party roots. Some grooms prefer not to call the party they have with their friends a bachelor party at all and instead see it as a chance to have some fun with their peers—college friends, old high school cliques, and other contemporaries—without having to consider the tastes and sensibilities of in-laws and elderly relatives.

If you do decide to have a traditional bachelor party,

what you do of course is up to you . . . mostly. Your best man should probably take the initiative to plan your bachelor party and will most likely have many surprises in store for your big night out. Don't be afraid to make your preferences known and draw some boundaries. If you have no interest in going to a strip club, say so, and if crawling through the mud dodging paintball pellets is not your idea of a good time, let your best man know. If he's a good enough friend to be your best man, then he's probably a good enough friend to know and respect your wishes.

If fine dining is your bag, spend the night at an upscale steak house sipping Scotch and sampling porterhouse. Camping or fishing trips can be just the ticket for guys looking to get in touch with nature. Brewery tours, ski trips, or a day at the races might be what you are looking for. You might relive your glory days and head back to your alma mater for a bar crawl through all your favorite old spots.

Whether it lasts a weekend or a night, I would caution you against having your bachelor party too close to your wedding day. Whatever you do, you absolutely shouldn't have it the night before. Waking up with a hangover will make even walking down the aisle in a straight line an enormous challenge, and no amount of cologne will cover the stink of alcohol sweating through your pores. Never, never, never be hungover on your wedding day.

SO TAKE OFF ALL YOUR CLOTHES— STRIP CLUBS

Shortly before my bachelor party, an acquaintance at work asked about my plans and practically ordered me to go to a strip club. "Dude," he said, "you have to go." I was confused by his insistence. Is strip-club attendance mandatory for all grooms-to-be? When I apply for my marriage license, do I have to sign a notarized affidavit swearing that I paid $20 for a lap dance? Do Las Vegas airport officials not let you on the plane to go home unless you can prove you saw a naked breast during your trip?

My coworker explained the reasoning behind his zeal: "Dude, you have to say good-bye to all that." This confused me even more. To what would I be saying good-bye, exactly? Breast implants, bleach-bottle-blond dye jobs, and sequined G-strings? When had I ever said hello to *any* of that? If I had really needed to say good-bye to anything, I would have gone to a bar on the Upper East Side of Manhattan and gotten rejected by short, curly-haired girls carrying Kate Spade bags. That was something to which I was happy to say good-bye. Still, my friends were planning a Las Vegas trip for my bachelor party, and even though none of us wanted to take the advice of a guy who started every sentence with *dude*, we decided to follow the adage: when in Las Vegas, do as the Las Vegans do.

Leora had a mostly neutral opinion on the subject. She didn't have much of an issue with me going once for the bachelor party, but she didn't exactly want to be married to the type of guy who is as well-known at the local strip club as Norm is at Cheers. Women have, understandably, conflicting thoughts on strip clubs, ranging from those who are so blasé about it that they might even join their boyfriends or husbands at one to those who are adamantly against the very idea of women taking their clothes off for money.

The bachelor party and its related activities can be the biggest wedge issue of the entire wedding, so whatever you decide, be sensitive to your fiancée's wishes and, above all else, be honest. You would expect no less of her. In fact, think about how you would feel if the tables were turned. Are you completely comfortable with the idea of anonymous, scantily clad men gyrating in front of your wife-to-be for cash? The scenario is probably not even hypothetical, as your fiancée's friends may be planning a similarly styled bachelorette party for your bride when you are out with your friends.

Looking beyond the bachelor party, couples in trusting relationships should have what I would call a "Do ask, do tell" policy. A woman should feel comfortable asking her husband-to-be about everything without wondering if he is going to hold back or, in some cases, lie. And both people should expect the other to do the right thing no matter what the circumstances, even when in the company of ten or more alcohol-laden, judgment-impaired buddies. I would suspect that people who feel they have to police their partner's behavior have bigger problems than a discomfort with lap dances.

I did offer Leora some assurances before my departure for Las Vegas. I wouldn't have any women back to my room to "party" with me and my friends, I wouldn't drain my bank account on $20 lap dances and watered-down drinks, and I wouldn't run off to the Little White Chapel to marry a dancer named Bambi. I would, however, come home to Leora and tell her all about my trip. All of it. We have our own "Do ask, do tell" policy, but we also have another rule called "Look but don't touch." Luckily for any women worried about their fiancés, the strip clubs have the same policy.

I AM WOMAN, HEAR ME OPINE—
WOMEN TALK ABOUT STRIP CLUBS

Any debate about strip clubs could fill a book. So, rather than rattle on myself, I decided to ask a random sampling of women what they think. Here they are, in their own words.

> *I don't personally understand the hubbub a lot of women make over strip clubs. I get it; dudes like naked chicks. Ooh, big mystery, boobs. Whatever. Hanging at a strip club once in a while with the guys shouldn't be equated with cheating or dumped on too hard.*
> *—Jen, Chicago, Illinois*

> *We should let our significant other hear our real opinions no matter how "stiff" they sound, especially if it crosses our boundaries on what we call personal between one another. I cannot for the life of me understand the need to look at other naked women and have them rub their bodies all over them. If you feel the need to do that, you aren't satisfied at home and you shouldn't be getting married.*
> *—Mary, Milwaukee, Wisconsin*

I wouldn't exactly call strip clubs degrading, but I wouldn't exactly drive my fiancé down to the club either. He can go for his bachelor party if he wants, and I trust him enough to not worry about what happens.

—Susan, Los Angeles, California

Guys feel this need to act as manly as possible when put in a group with other guys. This might include talking about sports, eating, playing video games, or going to strip clubs. My fiancé has only gone to strip clubs for bachelor parties, and while I don't really like it, I know that he would only go to hang out with the guys and put on a more manly front. Probably my biggest problem I had with it is when he came home afterwards and I didn't want him to look at me. I jumped under the covers with my oversized T-shirt. While I know I have a nice figure, I just don't want him comparing me to the new images of women from the club. I want to be the prettiest woman he's ever seen, and it's hard to feel that I am if I don't know what he's seen.

—Robyn, Lindale, Texas

Personally, I am uncomfortable with the idea of strip clubs being the main event for a bachelor party. While I'm not lacking in confidence regarding our relationship, frankly, I don't see the point.

—Olivia, Richmond, Virginia

What's the big deal? Considering the amount of silicone on some of those women, they are no more real than the women my fiancé sees in movies and magazines. As long as

he comes home to me at the end of the night, I don't have a problem with him going at all. Heck, I'd even go with him.
—Staci, Atlanta, Georgia

Why would you do something just before getting married if you don't do it in your normal everyday life? If you buy into the "losing your freedom" concept, then you may act out and do something you wouldn't normally do. If my husband is going to act out, I'd prefer it if there weren't naked women around.
—Jamie Beth, New York, New York

I don't know what the big deal is. If he goes once, fine. If he goes twice, not so fine. If he goes a lot, big problem.
—Sari, St. Louis, Missouri

In most debates about strip clubs, one perspective that is usually not represented is that of those who work in the industry itself. Carrie (not her real name), a dancer in Las Vegas, doesn't exactly have advice for the concerned women waiting at home, but cautions partying bachelors from acting like complete buffoons in the name of one last hurrah. "It's called a gentlemen's club for a reason," she says. "If you're not going to act like one, go somewhere else."

Jennifer Yoffe, the events director of a popular strip club in New York City, offers this advice to women who are worried about their fiancé becoming attracted to someone after a lap dance. "Look at it from the entertainer's point of view. Do you really think she is thinking, 'I can't wait to work tonight so I can steal someone's husband'? Of course not!" Jennifer's view is understandably more businesslike. "What she is really thinking is 'I hope work is good tonight and some guy comes in here and gives me all his money for nothing.' So, ladies, the only thing you have to worry about isn't that your man will cheat, but that he'll spend too much money!"

ENGAGED GROOM TIP

For Your Guys Only?

Who should be invited to your bachelor party? The typical bachelor party, of course, is a group of guys who have long-standing and close ties to the man of the hour. But that doesn't mean that all of your close male friends and relatives should be invited. In fact, it may be more useful for you to think about who *shouldn't* be invited, rather than who should. Think twice about asking your future brother-in-law to attend, as neither of you may feel comfortable watching the other with a stripper on his lap or slurring his speech as he tries to order his tenth gin and tonic. It should go without saying that your father and future father-in-law are better off staying at home, especially if you're only used to seeing your father drink at Christmas or Passover. And just as you wouldn't want to make a fool of yourself at the office holiday party, you might not want to invite your boss or any coworkers to the bachelor party, unless you want tales of your drunken debauchery circulating around the watercooler on Monday morning.

Coed bachelor parties are not uncommon, although they may have a more subdued tone than the all-night stag party. It's perfectly reasonable to assume that you might have a lot of close female friends, so if you'd have a hard time dividing your friends by gender, going out for a big dinner with all of your amigos, male and female, is a great way to involve as many people as possible. Spike, a graduate student from New York, gave the traditional bachelor party a modern twist, spending the day playing paintball with his buddies, but ending the day at a bar where his fiancée and larger group of friends—male and female—shared drinks and stories.

Part Four

THE FINAL COUNTDOWN

The last four to six weeks before your wedding day fly by like no others before them. The better prepared you and your bride are for a potentially dizzying array of prenuptial errands and jobs, the more fun you'll have when the clock ticks down to zero.

Some of the tasks you may have left to do are minor and can be taken care of with the flip of a cell phone. Call your caterer with a final head count so he or she knows how many plates of chicken cordon bleu to have ready. If you reserved a block of hotel rooms for your guests and left a deposit or credit card number, make sure you release any empty rooms so you don't get charged. If you have made gift bags for your out-of-town guests, call the hotels and arrange for them to be dropped off before your first guests arrive. Talk to grandparents or any other elderly guests with special transportation needs and arrange to get them from the airport or their homes to the ceremony and reception.

If your bride has taken on the majority of the work so far, this is your last chance to step up. Believe me, she'll appreciate the help. Write a batch of thank-you notes for any presents you've received recently so you're ahead of the game before you leave on your honeymoon. Offer to clean your apartment, do the laundry, and drop off the dry cleaning so you'll have a clean home when you return from your vacation.

You might have a lot left to do. Your fiancée might be panicking about getting it done. To help alleviate the pressure, don't be afraid to call in a favor or take people up on any offers of assistance. You're an Engaged Groom, not Superman, and no one person can be expected to take on everything himself. The more things you and your bride can accomplish now and the more help you have, the less stress you're likely to feel as the big day approaches. When you wake up on your wedding day, how would you rather feel? Excited to begin a new chapter in your life or relieved that the whole wedding planning ordeal is finally over? Some couples spend so much time focusing on their wedding's details that they lose sight of the marriage they are about to begin.

Still, there are some important tasks left, perhaps more important than any you've dealt with so far. This section will guide you through these and offer some helpful hints on getting everything in order before the big day.

14

Confirming It All

Here's a true story. While it wasn't ripped from the headlines, all the names have been changed to protect the innocent.

On the day of Mike and Rhea's wedding, Scott, the best man, was assigned to wait outside the church to greet the florist, musicians, and photographer about one hour before the ceremony's start and usher them inside. Understanding that the bride and groom would be busy getting ready, Scott was more than happy to take on this task.

The florist arrived as scheduled, and Scott gave her directions on where to set up inside. A few minutes later the musicians pulled into the parking lot. Scott gave them a printed schedule, a list of songs to be played during the procession, and the names of people who were giving toasts at the reception. Everything seemed to be falling into place, but as the clock ticked down to the zero hour and as more guests started to arrive, Scott was still nervously pacing, waiting for the photographer. His anxiety even caused him to stop every person with a fancy camera hanging from his neck. Most of these people turned out to be relatives who simply liked taking pictures and had money to blow on expensive SLRs, leaving Scott even more disappointed and nervous. Was this photographer ever going to show up?

With fifteen minutes to go, the photographer had still not arrived. Scott asked the bride's father if he knew anything about the photographer. He didn't, and neither did her mother. None of the other wedding party members knew. No one, it seemed, could give Scott an answer. After asking everyone but the flower girls, Scott had no choice but to send the maid of honor inside the bride's dressing room to ask the bride herself.

Needless to say, the photographer's tardiness did not sit well with the bride, whose prewedding calm was suddenly disrupted by the Case of the Missing Shutterbug. How could a photographer, to whom she had given a hefty deposit over eight months ago, simply not show up for a job? This wasn't just any job, Rhea thought to herself, but a job that involved the most important day of her life.

With only ten minutes to go before the ceremony, Rhea sent her cousin Catherine with Scott back to the hotel to fetch the notebook in which she had written every vendor's contact information. (As Scott and Catherine drove back to the hotel, they both wondered why Rhea and Mike hadn't bothered to bring this notebook with them to the church in the first place.)

Risking life, limb, and a few extra points on his license, Scott raced back to the hotel, where he and Catherine found the notebook. Catherine called the photographer's office. No answer. Realizing that on a Saturday the photographer would probably be coming from home and not from an office, Scott and Catherine used their cell phones to call everyone in the phone book with the photographer's last name. After speaking with dozens of bewildered people, they had made no progress in tracking him down.

Scott and Catherine headed back to the church no wiser about the missing photographer. The ceremony was now almost thirty minutes behind schedule. With nearly two hundred guests waiting and ice sculptures melting at the country club down the street, Mike and Rhea made an executive decision. Word was discreetly passed to the family members with cameras that their amateur services would be needed. Groomsmen made requests of everyone holding a camera, from those with expensive digital shooters to those who had picked up a disposable on the way to the church.

The rest of the wedding and the reception went off without a hitch, and eventually Mike and Rhea would wind up with enough photographs from their friends and relatives to paste together a suitable album. The photographer never did show up, and with a plane to catch the day after their wedding so they could begin their honeymoon, Mike and Rhea would have to wait to find out why.

Scott, however, was still on the case. Back at home on Monday morning, he checked online for as much information about the photographer as he could find. Typing in the photographer's name and the name of the town where the wedding had been held, Scott was directed to the Web site for a local newspaper. There, he discovered the reason for the photographer's absence. Unfortunately, he found it among the newspaper's obituaries. The photographer had died two months before the wedding.

A story like this may be an extreme example, but if it teaches you anything, it should be this: *call every service provider within one week of your wedding for confirmation.*

Make sure that every vendor has reliable driving directions and knows exactly when to arrive. Call the reception hall and double-check the start time for your event. Don't simply tell your photographer when the ceremony begins, find out how long he'll need to set up and ask him to arrive with enough time to spare before he's supposed to start snapping pictures. Call your tailor to make sure your tuxedo will be available for pickup as scheduled. If a vendor did not receive a check or if you still have any payments outstanding, now is a good time to work all of those details out. You may not have to deal with dead photographers or AWOL florists, but taking a few minutes to confirm everything can give you a head start on dealing with any last-minute inconveniences.

15

Seating Assignments and Other Arrangements

One of the most challenging aspects of wedding planning, whether you are having twenty guests or two hundred, is making a seating chart. If you are having an extended cocktail hour or a less formal affair without any sort of assigned seating, consider yourself lucky—and skip ahead to the next chapter. Making a seating chart for a sit-down dinner is like building a house of cards, but instead of using cards you're using white folding chairs. You may feel as if the potential for disaster is enormous.

No family, even one as wholesome as the Waltons or as well adjusted as the Huxtables, is without its fair share of drama. Even if you aren't dealing with the delicate issue of divorced parents or icy-cool in-laws, you may have a group of friends who are in the midst of their own little civil war, making coming up with a viable seating chart as intricate a process as planning a major military campaign.

But like any good general, don't retreat from this responsibility. Nothing you've done so far as an Engaged Groom needs your involvement like making a seating chart. Why? Because no matter how much one person might want to take this on alone, it's too big a job for just your bride or your mother-in-law. There's no possible way either of them can know every last bit of your family's history. Your bride may never have heard the story of your dad's cousin Fred and how he once stole money from your mom's uncle Ralph. You might still be friendly with a few ex-girlfriends, but will your mother-in-law really know enough to seat them as far from each other as possible? Try to involve at least one of your parents, as your mother or father will have an even better idea of family feuds.

If all of this soap-opera-style drama makes you less than enthusiastic about getting involved, you could look at it from a different perspective. Making a seating chart is a great way for you and your bride to learn a little more about each other's colorful family history. At the least, you'll have a chance to familiarize yourself with everyone's name, increasing the chances that you'll recognize distant cousins and your legally inherited new family members when you see them at the reception.

The best way to make a seating chart is to really conceptualize the room. Your event space may be able to provide you with a floor map, but if not, draw one up yourself. Picture where each table will be set up and how they'll be spaced around a dance floor. Mark off space for the band, bar stations, or other food-service tables. Note all entrances and exits and the placement of bathrooms. You never know which guest will be offended by sitting too close to the men's room.

Stuart Rosenberg, the bandleader, recommends that you

seat your oldest guests as far away from a band's speakers as possible without exiling them to Siberia. The older the guest, the more likely he'll spend most of your wedding at his table, and you don't want anyone to waste the battery on his hearing aid. In all seriousness, it's a courtesy no different from providing a vegetarian meal for your non-meat-eating friends.

ENGAGED GROOM TIP

Do You Know Me?

Everyone knows how difficult it is to remember names at big events like weddings. In my experience, it's not uncommon to sit down at a table and introduce myself only to forget everyone's name before I unfold my napkin.

Just before Leora and I were about to have place cards printed, Leora's father suggested that we have them printed with each person's name on the front *and* back. That way people would be able to read the name of the person sitting across from them. Additionally, when making rounds at our wedding, Leora and I would easily be able to survey each table for a quick who's who. Seeing as how you'll have a number of relatives and friends whom you haven't seen in years coming to your wedding, this might save you the embarrassment of admitting that you can't remember a person's name. It's a tad tacky to have everyone wear "Hello, My Name Is" stickers on their lapels or evening dresses, so this suggestion was one of the best I heard in a year of wedding planning. And I'm not just saying that because I need to suck up to my father-in-law.

SAVE US A SEAT—WHERE DO YOU SIT?

After going to great lengths to come up with a seating chart that successfully balances the fragile egos of some of their guests, many brides and grooms forget to save seats for two important people: themselves. Others do it without much thought and wind up hurting someone's feelings. As if separating your Hatfields from your McCoys isn't difficult enough, how much thought do you have to give to seating the biggest wedding VIPs of 'em all?

You might decide to avoid any perceived slights entirely by having a small, two-person table set up in a central location. While some couples might balk at the idea of being separated from their families and friends, others find that they wind up spending so little time actually sitting down at their reception that not claiming two seats at a larger table is a great option.

Other couples choose to sit with immediate family members. At my wedding, Leora and I sat with my parents, her parents, her sister and brother-in-law, my grandmother, and her companion. With tables of ten scattered throughout the room, this worked perfectly. If your parents are divorced or you have an exceptionally large family, however, this may not work for you.

An easy solution to your seating dilemma is to just sit with the members of your wedding party. Anyone who isn't a groomsman or bridesmaid will already have seen those who were standing with you at your wedding and not give their seating assignment a second thought.

ENGAGED GROOM TIP

Let's Stay Together

Some couples set up one long table for the bride, groom, and members of the wedding party as if they are participating in some sort of Friars Club roast. If you choose this option, don't crowd out the dates of the people in your wedding party. Says one groom, who wishes to remain anonymous lest he offend the offending parties, "After traveling across the country last year for a wedding with my fiancée, I had to sit at the 'abandoned people table' while she sat up front and got served first. We're not doing a head table at our wedding for that reason, but I still considered seating the couple who did it to us at separate tables. I didn't consider it for very long, but I did have a good evil laugh to myself at the thought."

16

Your Wedding Day Schedule

You and your fiancée will be too busy—and perhaps too nervous—to answer a million questions about who needs to be where when on your wedding day. The more information you can get to those directly involved with your wedding, the more they will be able to fulfill their own roles without peppering you both with questions.

Talk with your bride and create a schedule of how you expect your wedding day to unfold. Do your groomsmen need to show up early to seat guests? Do the bridesmaids need to hang around after the ceremony to pose for pictures before heading over to the reception? Are there any special prewedding rituals for which you'd like your entire wedding party present? Having a mental picture of how your wedding day will be structured and then committing that picture to paper is a great way to take the edge off any prewedding jitters and can help you avoid any last-minute headaches like the one experienced by Mike and Rhea.

Such a schedule should include all event times and the key people expected to participate. You might find it to be a real logistical challenge, like building a house of cards, as moving around one event can often mean restructuring the entire schedule, depending on who needs to be involved. If you and your fiancée are superstitious about seeing each other before the wedding starts, for example, you may need to schedule certain prewedding activities in different locations, adding another twist to your scheduling task. (For formal portraits, your photographer should be able to give you a sample schedule based on one of the many weddings he's done before.)

For example:

SUNDAY, AUGUST 29TH

Ceremony: Temple Emmanuel
123 Main Street
Oconomowoc
(262) 555-1212

Reception: Lake View Country Club,
1459 Lac La Belle Drive,
Oconomowoc
(262) 555-2121

TIME	EVENT	LOCATION	PARTICIPANTS
10:00 A.M.	Wedding party arrives	Temple Emmanuel	Wedding party, Kaye & Gordon families
10:15	Bridesmaids' pictures	Temple courtyard	Leora, bridesmaids
10:30	Groomsmen's pictures	Temple main entrance	Doug, groomsmen
11:00 A.M.	*Ketubah* signing	Temple reception room	Everyone
11:45	Lineup	Back hall	Everyone
12:00 noon	**Ceremony**	Main chapel	Everyone
12:45	Leora & Doug pictures	Temple courtyard	Leora, Doug
12:55	Marriage license signing	Back hall	Rabbi Rigler Jay, Shelly
1:00 P.M.	**Cocktail hour**	Lake View Country Club—terrace	
2:00 P.M.	**Reception**	Lake View Country Club—main event room	

Include a list of important cell phone numbers—yours, your best man's, your fiancée's maid of honor, etc.—so that anyone who is running late can either call or be tracked down.

Be as detailed as you think you need to be to help your event flow as smoothly as possible. Some people might even micromanage the reception, breaking it up into courses or scheduling toasts and the cake-cutting ceremony for specific times. Others might keep such information limited to discussions with the caterer and the bandleader, preferring a more natural flow.

It should go without saying, but have your schedule available to your wedding party—family members, groomsmen, bridesmaids, and your officiant—in advance by either having it waiting for them when they check into their hotels or by passing it out at your rehearsal dinner. You can also post this information on your wedding Web site, although you might want to put it in a section accessible only to the wedding party, immediate family members, and other people who are directly involved in the ceremony. Whatever you do, don't wait until the last minute. A schedule calling for your groomsmen to show up two hours before the ceremony is worthless if they don't get it until after you need them there.

ENGAGED GROOM TIP

10-4, Good Buddy

My wedding was spread out over a large, campuslike area, meaning that the likelihood of any two people being in the same place at the same time was fairly slim. Worried about cell phone reception inside buildings and in other off-the-beaten-path locations, we bought inexpensive walkie-talkies and gave one to each person in our wedding party. This allowed everyone to stay in touch and meant that some of our friends, who are notorious for never being in the right place at the right time, would always know what was going on. Rather than fixing stragglers with ankle bracelets or sending out a search party to the restroom to track down MIA bridesmaids, we put out a call over the walkie-talkies.

17

Marriage Licenses and Blood Tests

A marriage license is simply a permit issued by the state allowing you to get married. Even if you have a marriage license in hand, you will not be legally married until a ceremony—be it religious or civil—is performed by a qualified officiant. On the flip side, most religious leaders and other officiants won't marry you and your fiancée without the proper legal approval.

On an individual level, your license has little practical purpose. You won't have to present it for identification purposes at R-rated movies and won't get asked to show it along with your registration when a cop pulls you over for speeding. Once signed by your officiant and witnesses and certified by the local county clerk's office or other government office, your marriage license or certificate will, however, come in handy and be quite necessary for a number of things. You'll need it if you add your new wife to your health insurance plan, for example, and are required to provide proof of your date of marriage. If your fiancée is planning to change her name sometime after your wedding, having a certified copy of your wedding certificate is the only way to make sure the process flows as smoothly as possible. Most of the time, however, the piece of paper on which your license is printed will live inside a bank safe-deposit box or file folder at home.

Nevertheless, the law is the law, and the methods, waiting periods, fees, and other rules for issuing marriage licenses vary so much from state to state and county to county that any advice on getting one can read like the fine print on a sweepstakes. *All the information included in this section is subject to change, so do your homework by calling your local issuing authority.*

In most states you will go to a county clerk's office or city administrative office to apply for your license. Some states issue licenses valid statewide, but others have more restrictive geographic requirements. In Wisconsin, where Leora and I were married, out-of-towners must apply in the county in which their ceremony will take place, but residents can apply in the county in which they live.

No matter where you have to go, give yourself the proper amount of time to apply for and receive your license. Processing your application can take a few days, and you'd hate to apply for your wedding license the Friday before your Sunday wedding only to find that you'll have to wait four business days to pick it up. Many states have different definitions of the word *day,* defining it as either a full twenty-four hours, a business day, or a mere passing from one calendar date to the next. (You should also check to see if state offices are closed for any legal holidays before you apply.)

But don't give yourself too much time. In states such as

Georgia and New Mexico, a marriage license never expires, but in most places the clock starts ticking as soon as you leave the county clerk's office. Most states have strict expiration periods for wedding licenses, and they're not exactly something you can renew over and over. If you are getting married in New Jersey, for example, and apply for your marriage license six weeks before your wedding, you'll wind up having to submit another application within two weeks of the big day.

If you're in a pinch and didn't plan ahead, you might still be in luck. Some states waive waiting periods for active-duty military personnel, although I wouldn't recommend enlisting in the Marines just to catch a break on your wedding license. In-state residents are sometimes subject to shorter waiting periods than out-of-towners, and in some cases those who take premarriage counseling courses through a state-approved psychologist or therapist can get a marriage license with no wait at all. In some extreme cases, judges can waive the waiting period and grant a license. If all else fails, just hope that you are getting married in a place where you can have your application expedited for an additional fee.

MARRIAGE LICENSE WAITING PERIODS AND EXPIRATIONS BY STATE*

STATE	WAITING PERIOD	LICENSE EXPIRATION
Alabama	None	30 days
Alaska	3 days	90 days
Arizona	None	1 year
Arkansas	None	60 days
California	None	90 days
Colorado	None	30 days
Connecticut	None	65 days
Delaware	1 day	30 days
Florida	3 days	60 days
Georgia	None	Never
Hawaii	None	30 days
Idaho	None	Never
Illinois	1 day	60 days
Indiana	None	60 days
Iowa	3 days	60 days
Kansas	3 days	6 months
Kentucky	None	30 days
Louisiana	3 days	30 days

*Information on this list is subject to change. Check with your state or local government.

STATE	WAITING PERIOD	LICENSE EXPIRATION
Maine	None	90 days
Maryland	2 days	6 months
Massachusetts	3 days	60 days
Michigan	3 days	30 days
Minnesota	5 days	6 months
Mississippi	None	30 days
Missouri	3 days	30 days
Montana	None	180 days
Nebraska	None	1 year
Nevada	None	1 year
New Hampshire	3 days	90 days
New Jersey	3 days	30 days
New Mexico	None	Never
New York	1 day	60 days
North Carolina	None	60 days
North Dakota	None	60 days
Ohio	None	60 days
Oklahoma	None	30 days
Oregon	3 days	60 days
Pennsylvania	3 days	60 days
Rhode Island	None	90 days

STATE	WAITING PERIOD	LICENSE EXPIRATION
South Carolina	1 day	Never
South Dakota	None	20 days
Tennessee	None	30 days
Texas	3 days	30 days
Utah	None	30 days
Vermont	None	60 days
Virginia	None	60 days
Washington	3 days	60 days
Washington, DC	5 days	Never
West Virginia	None	60 days
Wisconsin	6 days	30 days
Wyoming	None	Never

What do you have to bring with you when you apply for your marriage license? It should go without saying, but the most important thing to remember is your bride. Both of you will be required to be present at the time of your application. Bring proper identification such as a driver's license or passport, birth certificate, Social Security card, and even a recent utility bill, mortgage statement, or apartment lease if proof of residency is required.

Like the best things in life, marriage licenses are, unfortunately, not free. Fees can range from as low as $15 or $20 to over $100. The state in which you will be married might charge different fee structures for residents and out-of-towners, but sometimes only one-half of a couple needs to be a resident to qualify for a lower fee. Many licensing offices will only accept cash, money orders, or checks, so make sure you bring not only the right amount of money, but also the proper form of payment.

If you have any skeletons in your closet, such as an ex to whom you are secretly sending alimony or a second wife and four kids stashed away on the other side of town, now might be a good time to come clean. Most marriage applications will ask for your marital history and the name of any ex-spouses, and there isn't a state in the union that allows bigamy.

This is also a good time to talk with your fiancée about her married name, or, for more progressive couples, your married name. If she plans to take your name or if you plan to hyphenate or change your surnames altogether, you may need to indicate that on your marriage license and file all accompanying legal paperwork soon.

No matter what your state's requirements, be sure to sign and date your marriage license and have it signed immediately following your ceremony by your officiant and any required witnesses before it is sent back to a state or county office for an official seal of approval. Talk with your priest, rabbi, or other officiant about who is responsible for mailing in or dropping off your signed marriage license after the wedding. Your best man or your bride's maid of honor can also step up for this job.

THIS WILL ONLY HURT FOR
A SECOND—BLOOD TESTS

Anyone with a needle phobia will be happy to learn that only a handful of states—Connecticut, Georgia, Indiana, Massachusetts, Mississippi, Montana, and Oklahoma, as well as Washington, DC, as of this writing—still require any form of blood or medical testing as part of the marriage license application. Such tests typically screen for common sexually transmitted and infectious diseases and must be administered by a state-sanctioned lab or medical office within thirty days or less of your marriage license application's filing. Some states only require that your fiancée get tested for rubella. Still others only ask that you sign a document saying you've received and read pamphlets or brochures on STDs, genetic health, or other public health issues, which is always a good alternative to rolling up your sleeve.

18

Wedding Rings

When you bought your fiancée's engagement ring, you undoubtedly learned a lot about jewelry, perhaps more than you ever knew before. After learning about color, clarity, cut, and carats and the differences between platinum and white gold, you hardly need a book to tell you how to pick out your wedding rings.

Still, your wedding ring will be a whole lot different from your fiancée's engagement ring. For starters, you're the one who'll have to wear this one, so this time around your taste and comfort actually matter. Since this might be the first and last piece of jewelry you ever wear, choose carefully.

Ask any guy who just got married, and he'll tell you that he's constantly playing with his ring. It might help to put your ring on and wear it around the house before your wedding if you're nervous about how it might feel. You'll soon get used to it, but that doesn't mean you won't notice it's there. For months after my wedding, I slid my ring on and off my finger, tapped it against tables, and twisted it around my knuckle. I don't mind wearing it at all, but the sensation of having it on all the time is something that took some time to get used to. In fact, some guys find that it takes a long time. "After eight years, I still play with my ring," says JT, a biologist from Oakland, California.

Unlike the last time you went ring shopping, this time your fiancée will definitely come with you. You don't have to pick out matching rings—she may want something bejeweled and engraved while you may opt for a simple band of metal—but some couples find that, at the least, complementary rings are romantic.

Traditionally, the groom pays for his bride's wedding ring and the bride pays for his. Like any gifts, you may want to keep the prices of your rings a secret from each other. But if you are splitting the cost or if the payment is coming from a joint bank account, talk with your fiancée about how much you plan to spend before you go to the diamond district or hit the mall. You may already have a line item in your budget to cover the cost of the rings, but if you haven't accounted for this expense yet, do it soon. Calculating what you can afford while under the watchful eye of a commission-hungry salesperson can almost be as stressful as buying a new car.

If you are having a religious ceremony, ask your officiant about any requirements or restrictions that may influence your rings' style. Jewish law, for example, requires that a wedding ring be unadorned and free from any engravings, symbolic of the perfect union that marriage is intended to create.

When you finally do go shopping, ask how long it will take before the rings are ready. Most jewelers will have what you want on the spot and can size a ring for you quickly at no additional cost, but if you are ordering something special or having your rings engraved, it could take a few weeks at least or even a couple of months. You can forget a lot of things on your wedding day and most of them can be replaced, but finding a stand-in for the rings you and your bride want to be married in and wear the rest of your lives is not easy.

If you are ordering a unique ring with intricate designs or are having your ring engraved, you may want to ask the jeweler if resizing it later will be a problem. If you gain or lose a lot of weight years into your marriage, you may risk ruining a special pattern or inscription if you need to get your ring resized.

ENGAGED GROOM TIP

Put the Man in Manicure

Along with a nice haircut, a fresh shower, and a close shave, one other thing should be at the top of any groom's grooming checklist: a manicure.

You read that correctly. Of all the last-minute details you'll be concentrating on before your wedding day, it might feel strange to focus on as small a detail as your fingernails, especially if you've never had a manicure before. But if ever there was a time to start thinking about cuticles and nail beds, that time is now.

Why? To answer this question, let's consider some

other questions, shall we? When you presented your fiancée with a sparkling new engagement ring, how many people grabbed her hand and demanded to see her new bling? What do you think will happen to you once a ring has been placed on your finger?

It won't matter if you are opting for a plain gold band or even a loop of neatly folded tinfoil. Everyone at your reception will want to see it, either to satisfy his or her curiosity about its value or simply to confirm that you are, in fact, married. While people might not notice your professionally manicured fingers, they will notice a dirty hangnail. A good manicure can even cover up your nasty nervous habit of chewing your nails.

If you are concerned about being the only man in some frilly *Steel Magnolias*–like salon, don't be. Many men's salons offer nail services for their clientele, and unlike the manicures your fiancée might get, yours will be a quick file and buff with only a minimal amount of lotion and chemicals.

19

One Last Breath before Taking the Plunge

Even if you and your bride have been fairly autonomous in decision-making, all of those decisions have probably involved a cast of dozens, from a caterer and DJ to even your family and future in-laws. If you've been keeping up with your regular date nights, congratulations. You're now ready for the most important date night of them all.

A few days before your wedding—or one or two nights before you get on a plane if your wedding is taking place away from your current home—reserve your fiancée for your last date as an unmarried couple. Even though it may feel as if there is still too much to do and no matter what demands other people are making of you, you can certainly spare two or three hours to spend some time alone with your bride-to-be.

This date can be as simple or elaborate as time—and your wallet—will allow. Revisit the site of your first date or head back to the spot where you proposed. Make a reservation at your favorite restaurant. Take a stroll down memory lane and flip through old photo albums. Take a literal drive through your favorite parts of town or visit an area that has special significance, such as a park or your old apartment building. Cook dinner together at home and open that bottle of wine you've been saving for a special occasion.

You might not have time for a weekend at a beach house or an overnight camping trip, but taking even just a few hours to do something special together can help keep you and your bride focused on each other before the onslaught of the multitudes: the friends and family members who, at this very moment, are getting ready to attend your wedding.

FROM ME TO YOU—WEDDING PRESENTS FOR YOUR BRIDE

In addition to the mixers, wineglasses and bedsheets you've received from your friends and family, traditionally you and your bride will exchange gifts before your wedding day. Some couples match the magnitude of their wedding day's meaning with a gift of high value, spending the last pennies in their bank accounts to follow this tradition. But after all the money you've spent on an engagement ring, wedding rings, or the wedding itself, you may find this to be not only unnecessary but prohibitively expensive as well.

Even if your budget is stretched to the breaking point, that doesn't mean you have to abandon the practice of getting each other something special. Some couples save their money for their honeymoon, seeing it as a present they can enjoy together. Others pick a weekend one year from their wedding date and in the interim save money for an anniversary weekend trip to a bed-and-breakfast or beachside hotel. More immediately, you could give your bride an inexpensive gift certificate to her favorite clothing store so she can pick something to wear on your honeymoon. Even if you and your bride have promised not to buy each other gifts, buy a romantic card in which you declare your love, devotion, and excitement for the step you are about to take. At the very least, say it with flowers.

And don't forget your parents and future in-laws. They probably deserve some recognition for their role in either paying for or supporting your wedding efforts.

ENGAGED GROOM TIP

From A to Zzzzzz's

This is it. Everything on your checklists and to-do lists has been checked and done. After months of budgeting, reservation making, scheduling, menu planning, there isn't one thing left you need to do other than shower, shave, and show up. You're done.

Or are you? There's still one thing left to do, something so simple that most grooms overlook it entirely.

Get a good night's sleep.

Depending on how nervous you are, this might be the hardest task yet. Your buddies might want to take you out for one last night of freedom, as if your impending marriage will end with you sold into slavery and shipped to another country, never to be seen again. One more drink with your pals can easily turn into five, and the last thing you would want is to feel hungover on your wedding day. Resist the perilous pull of peer pressure. The night before my wedding, one of the hardest things I had to do was tell my friends, who hadn't all been in the same room at the same time since college, that I had to go to bed.

Set a curfew for yourself and stick to it. Even if your idea of "sleeping" is to get into bed and stare at the ceiling, getting as much rest as you can before your wedding day will help you save your energy for what is sure to be a fun, exciting, and, truth be told, exhausting day. After all, it's the biggest day of your life (so far).

Part Five

THE BIGGEST DAY OF YOUR LIFE (SO FAR)

Why the qualifier? Why isn't this section called "The Biggest Day of Your Life" period? Because in a life that might see any number of job promotions, the births of children and grandchildren, or, in your wildest fantasies, the acceptance of a World Series trophy, Academy Award, or large lottery prize, the coming years will be filled with plenty of big days. So don't listen to anyone who tells you it doesn't get any bigger than your wedding day. After all, if this is the biggest day of your life, does that mean that it's all downhill from here?

That's not to say that your wedding day won't be huge, if not in its execution then at least in the way it lives on in your memory. Even the most un-Engaged Groom will tell you that his wedding was something special. Seeing your bride as she walks down the aisle in her dress for the first time is a moment you can never duplicate. The smiles on your parents' faces and the tears in your grandparents' eyes are moments worthy of every greeting card ever written in the history of man.

For perhaps more than a year, you've been involved with every big decision and a lot of small ones. You've been an Engaged Groom par excellence, and when you wake up on your wedding day—if you are able to sleep the night before—you will be officially done with planning the wedding. Your only job will be to focus on having a good time.

I know what you're thinking: easier said than done. With so many butterflies in your stomach or outright panic attacks about late-arriving photographers or last-minute thunderstorms ruining your picturesque outdoor wedding, it can be difficult to keep your focus. After months of having control over every choice, you and your bride are now at the mercy of Mother Nature, a dozen different wedding vendors, and, most terrifyingly of all, hundreds of your closest friends and family.

One thing that might be gnawing at you and your bride is that even with months of planning, you were never able to work out every last detail of your wedding. As the hour draws nearer, you both might start having mini–panic attacks. So what if you never told someone to fold the napkins like origami swans? Who cares if you can't remember if you asked the caterer to bring Coke instead of Pepsi? Are you really going to let any of these things affect your enjoyment of your wedding day? There is a showbiz adage that a bad dress rehearsal means a perfect performance. Even if you've never seen a Broadway show, I suggest you take this saying to heart.

No matter what the storybooks say, no matter how happy the brides and grooms look in the pages of glossy magazines, it's not a question of *whether* something will go wrong on your wedding day, but *how* you will react when something goes awry. If the button on your tuxedo pants pops, it's not the end of the world. Find a safety pin, cover it up with a cummerbund, and you're as good as new. Even if the caterer drops a plate of food on a guest or the band mistakenly plays a song on your Do Not Play List, one fact remains: you'll still be married.

Think of the best wedding stories you've ever heard, and I'll bet that none of them begins with the sentence "Everything went exactly according to plan and we had no problems whatsoever." The best weddings, of course, are always perfect in their imperfection.

ENGAGED GROOM TIP

Eat Something, Will Ya?

If you are able to sleep the night before your wedding, congratulations. You have nerves of steel and are clearly ready for anything. Regardless of how you sleep, be sure to have something to eat when you wake up. Of all the days to skip breakfast, your wedding day is not one of them. Not that you should have a Grand-Slam meal of eggs, bacon, pancakes, and buttered toast, but eat at least a little food before you get ready. You'll need the energy to keep you going throughout the day, and it might just be the last bite of food you get until after it's all over. (More on that later.)

A GROOM'S CHECKLIST— EMERGENCY PROVISIONS

Since no one can anticipate exactly what you might need on your wedding day, pack a small bag containing the following and you'll be ready for every possible personal problem and may just have enough left over to survive a blizzard or nuclear war. It may feel a little strange to bring what amounts to a man purse to your wedding, but doing so will prevent anyone from having to make a last-minute run to a drugstore or back to your hotel room.

Personal Care

Water bottle
Toothpaste, toothbrush, dental floss, and
   mouthwash
Mints, gum, breath spray, etc.

Extra contact lenses and solution
Cologne
Brush or comb
Hair gel
Aspirin or other pain medication
Upset stomach/heartburn/indigestion medication
Chap Stick
Tissues
Nongreasy sunblock and bug repellent (for outdoor
   weddings)

Fashion Emergencies

Sewing kit (with thread to match the color of your
   clothing)
Lint brush
Change of clothes for after reception
Bag for returning rented formalwear (include a note
   with the rental company's address and phone
   number if you are handing this off to your best
   man or a family member before you leave for your
   honeymoon)

Miscellaneous

Cell phone and charger
Wallet with driver's license, credit cards, and cash
Extra set of keys for car, home, or hotel

Logistical Concerns

You might also want to prepare a small folder or large envelope with the following and give it to your best man or a responsible family member for safekeeping during your ceremony and reception.

Marriage license
A copy of prewritten vows
Copies of contracts for caterer, photographer, and
    other vendors
Contact numbers for all service providers
Payment for all service providers
Cash for gratuities
Cash and blank checks for miscellaneous expenses
Pen

If you bring nothing else, don't forget the first item on this list, your marriage license. Following the letter of the law, your officiant and at least one witness will need to sign it on the day of your wedding, or you won't be legally married. (Follow your local jurisdiction's licensing instructions carefully.)

20

The Ceremony

You don't need a guidebook to walk you through every element of the ceremony, as the various cultural requirements and traditions are so numerous that they could fill an entire book themselves. If you're having a religious ceremony, you'll go over some basic procedural aspects in prewedding meetings with a priest or rabbi. If you're having a civil ceremony that will be presided over by a family friend such as a judge or—if you are getting married on *The Love Boat*—a ship's captain, make sure to meet with that person well in advance of your wedding so you can go over the day's events. Hopefully the rehearsal dinner held the night before your wedding will be preceded by an actual rehearsal, though some weddings don't require too much preparation. After all, how hard is it to walk down an aisle?

Because weddings are such a common part of pop culture, exploited for entertainment on reality shows and showing up in TV season finales and the climaxes of romantic comedies, many of us think we know exactly what our wedding will look like. But like most things that come out of Hollywood, the fantasy rarely matches the reality. The last word of the phrase "love, honor, and obey" not only is outdated for today's egalitarian relationships, but doesn't even appear in the majority of wedding ceremonies. Weaned on decades of movie and TV weddings, some Jewish couples are surprised to find that they won't say the words "I do" at all and instead recite phrases in Hebrew that have been a part of that religion's wedding ceremony for thousands of years.

Still, no matter what religion you do or don't follow, there are some common elements, traditions, and concerns that come into play for all brides and grooms. Some are based on real truths, while others are simply relics from every Julia Roberts movie ever made. Knowing the distinction between the two can help you and your bride have the best ceremony possible.

CHOOSING SIDES—WHERE DO YOUR GUESTS SIT?

Most movie weddings take place in small, Norman Rockwell–esque churches with rows of wooden pews bisected by an aisle, dividing guests into two distinct groups: those who know the couple through the groom's side and those who are attending because they are friends of the bride's family. It is certainly still common practice for ushers to ask guests as they are seated, "Bride or groom?" However, don't think that because you've seen it done at other weddings, it's a requirement for yours.

While your immediate families might sit on one side or the other—or, in many cases, stand alongside you—there is nothing written in any great wedding manual that says your other guests must follow suit. In fact, it may feel somewhat arbitrary for your guests to separate themselves into two opposing teams. With many couples getting married later in life, it's also a possibility that your friends know you and your bride equally well. Having them make a quick decision about where their true loyalties lie after being prompted by an usher to choose between bride and groom might make your friends feel uncomfortable. If you are having a religious ceremony, talk with your officiant about what is common practice and whether it's something you should continue to observe. Most religious leaders will care more about starting the ceremony on time. As long as everyone is sitting down when they are supposed to, he or she won't probably care where they sit.

ARE YOU LOOKING AT ME?—SEEING YOUR BRIDE BEFORE THE WEDDING

Much of the idea that the bride and groom not see each other before the wedding is rooted in superstition, but some of it comes from more practical concerns. In the days of arranged marriages, the father of a bride and the father of a groom might agree to keep their children separated until the last possible moment, lest minor things such as love and physical attraction get in the way of what was essentially a business agreement between two men. Let's face it, if you had an ugly daughter and were living in medieval Europe, you wouldn't probably want anyone to see her until she was safely married off and out of the house, either.

But even though most brides and grooms today get to know each other over months and years, traditions die hard, and most people hold on to this one because they think it is what they are supposed to do. Remember, except for following the law of the state in which you are getting married, there is little you are *supposed* to do. Choosing to follow this tradition is up to you and your bride.

Some grooms like the idea of being surprised by their bride's appearance at the end of an aisle at the back of a church or function hall. The moment of seeing the bride for the first time in her dress, when all eyes are trained on her and she is truly the center of attention like at no other time, is hard to duplicate. If the idea of keeping that memory as pure and exciting as possible rings true for you and your bride, keeping yourselves away from each other before the ceremony is something you should choose.

In some ways, seeing your bride before the ceremony can make things easier for both of you. Even if you are surrounded by people who are already married, you might feel very much alone in the moments before your wedding, as no one will ever be able to know exactly how you are feeling at that moment. Having a moment to reflect with the person who is your partner on such a strange and exciting day can help calm even the most nervous temperaments. (At the least, seeing each other before the ceremony might give you time to pose for formal pictures, which will save you time later at the reception.)

There may be practical reasons why you and your bride see each other before the wedding. In Jewish weddings where a *ketubah*, or marriage contract, is signed before the wedding ceremony, both the bride and the groom and all witnesses must be present. Some couples, wishing to have pictures taken before tears of joy ruin a bride's makeup or before sweat lines a groom's brow, pose for a few pictures together before the ceremony.

So go ahead and see your bride before the ceremony, if she agrees. Don't worry about tradition or what anyone tells you. Whether you make a conscious decision to do it or stumble across your bride by accident, seeing each other before you get married will not send you to divorce court before your fifth anniversary.

ENGAGED GROOM TIP

The Rings, Please

Ask one thousand best men their biggest fear, and they'll all give the same answer: forgetting the wedding rings. In a ceremony involving dozens of family members and friends, big dresses, fancy tuxedos, and a learned religious leader, losing two tiny bands of metal—even precious metal—is a fear that's well-founded. So what can you do to minimize the risk that your best man—or father or brother-in-law or whoever has been charged with the responsibility— will have to leave in the middle of the ceremony to drive back to the hotel for the rings?

First of all, place both of the rings in one box and

leave the empty one at home. Having to keep track of two boxes doubles the chances that one of them might get lost, and the security that comes from knowing the rings are nestled snuggly together in one place is a nice metaphor for your marriage. But if your best man is still nervous about holding two items of substantial sentimental, financial, and, for the sake of your ceremony, practical value, there are other options.

Many weddings involve a variety of accessories such as wine cups, personal Bibles, or candles that are placed on a small table by the person performing your wedding. If, before the wedding begins, someone places the rings on this table, they will be there when you and your bride get to the end of the aisle. (Talk with your priest, rabbi, or other wedding officiant before doing this.)

If having a close friend hand you your rings is important to you, but your best man is still paranoid about losing the rings, use a safety pin to secure both rings to the inside of his tuxedo or suit. The few seconds it will take him to unhook the pin is a minor delay when compared to the steps he might have to retrace if he loses two unsecured rings through a tiny hole in his pocket.

In the Jewish faith, a wedding ring is supposed to be free of any engravings, diamonds, or other jewels; a solid metal band is all that is required. Many couples, however, prefer to have a decorated ring for everyday use and for that reason buy or borrow simple, unadorned rings for the ceremony. Imagine being a best man in a Jewish wedding; you might be responsible for four rings!

VOW OR NEVER—WRITING YOUR OWN VOWS

If there is time and space for it in your wedding ceremony, you and your bride may decide to write your own vows. Check with your officiant first, as some religious requirements may leave little space for self-written vows.

While you will probably want most of what you say to be a surprise to your bride, you and she should talk beforehand about some general vow-writing basics. For how long will each of you speak? Will your vows take a religious or more secular tone? Are there any details you absolutely don't want revealed in front of your friends and family or under the watchful eyes of God?

There is a reason this section is titled "Writing Your Own Vows," and it should be taken to heart. Whatever you plan to say to your bride in front of your friends and family should be written down on paper, not scribbled on your hand two minutes before the ceremony or written on a napkin with a borrowed pen. Even the most confident public speaker sometimes blows a few synapses between his brain and his mouth, and the last thing you want as you get ready to declare your undying love to your bride is to come up empty and draw a total blank. Writing your vows in advance can also prevent the opposite, which is being so verbose that you bore your guests to sleep. Don't worry about how reading from a set of index cards will look to your guests. If your words and feelings are genuine, most people will hardly care how they are presented.

FACT OR FICTION—SPEAK NOW OR FOREVER HOLD YOUR PIECE

In a little white church on a beautiful spring afternoon, a wedding ceremony nears its completion. A blushing bride and gushing groom stare lovingly into each other's eyes, only seconds away from being pronounced husband and wife by a gray-haired minister, who turns to address the congregation. "If anyone here can show just cause why this man and woman should not be married," he says, "speak now or forever hold your piece." Just then a jilted lover steps forward, proclaims his love for the bride, and, to the surprise of all those assembled and the horror of the groom, carries her out of the church. It could be a scene right out of *The Graduate* or a Julia Roberts movie. It might make for great drama, but could it happen to you?

Not likely. Beseeching a congregation to testify to the legitimacy of a couple's marriage was once commonplace in medieval Europe, where common life-cycle events— including births, weddings, deaths, and tax payments—were announced to the public. Called a banns, this announcement made sure that the community, which might include a large number of interrelated people, prevented consanguineous marriages.

Today, we live in a country of 280 million people, not a village of 280, and the chances that you might accidentally marry your cousin are statistically improbable. Any other legal barriers to marriage—a secret wife stashed away across town or a divorce that never went through—would most likely have been discovered during the application process when you obtained your marriage license. Some religions, such as Catholicism, still include the practice, but couples often request that it be removed in favor of more love-affirming declarations.

In the Jewish faith, a couple signs a *ketubah*, or marriage contract, that historically dictated the terms of the marriage before the wedding and prevented any last-minute surprises. (Today it is more of a declaration of love and commitment than a legal agreement.) Additionally, during a ceremony called the *bedeken*, a Jewish groom takes the responsibility of veiling his bride himself to avoid a mistake told of in the Bible. Jacob, who works seven years to earn the hand of La-ban's daughter Rachel, is tricked into marrying Laban's less attractive daughter Leah, who is hidden under a veil. Jacob doesn't realize his mistake until after the marriage is con-summated. From this story, some believe, a tradition was born.

With so many religious and legal checks and balances leading up to the modern wedding, the need for any last-minute theatrics has become a quaint remnant of a simpler time . . . and a staple of afternoon soap operas.

SEALED WITH A KISS—YOUR MOST PUBLIC DISPLAY OF AFFECTION

If there's one tradition that holds true across just about every religion and culture, it's that the wedding ends with a kiss.

It's also one tradition that makes a lot of grooms nervous, because it's not just any kiss, but *the* kiss. You know, *the* kiss that is done with all of your closest friends and family looking on. While you certainly don't need anyone to tell you how to kiss your bride—and if you do, I suggest going to a different section of the bookstore—just be sure to toe a thin line between taste and tackiness. You definitely wouldn't want the kiss you and your new wife exchange at the end of your wedding ceremony to be so devoid of passion that everyone starts worrying about your sex life, but neither do you want to deliver a saliva-drenched, tongue-wagging smacker worthy of the best late-night Cinemax has to offer. Aim for short and sweet and save the heavy stuff for the honeymoon suite.

21

The Reception

Only a wedding would have two events as different as different could be. A ceremony, even at its most joyous, is still a solemn occasion, and you will likely find yourself standing still for an hour or more as you take your vows and listen to a priest, rabbi, or other officiant perform the rites and rituals of your wedding. But suddenly, as soon as the ceremony is over, your wedding will transform into a frenzy of celebratory energy: the reception. You'll find yourself moving around like never before, either on the dance floor or between tables as you chat with old friends and family. More will happen at this party than you will probably ever remember, so just relax and do your best to soak it all in.

One of the most important things to remember at your reception is that you are there with your wife. Yes, your wife. Gone is the label *girlfriend* or *fiancée*. It's not just a new word, but also a whole new way of looking at the woman you love. It can feel a little weird at first, so test it out. Wife. Rhymes with *life*. Repeat after me. Wife. Very good.

As husband and wife you'll enjoy the party so much more if you experience it together. You don't necessarily have to be attached at the hip—your ceremony was not a conjoining surgery—but walk around together, dance together, eat together, and take time during the party to check in with each other. The sights, sounds, and smells of your wedding reception are bound to overwhelm you at times, so do your best to stay focused and enjoy every minute. This is one party you don't want to miss.

PLEASED TO MEET YOU— BEING A GOOD HOST

Few grooms, even the most painfully shy or the ones for whom the term *wallflower* was invented, have a hard time being social on their wedding day. How could it be any other way? You're at a party where everyone is there to honor you and your bride. As one-half of the center of attention, you'll have no problem finding things to talk about with your friends and family. Even if you're terrified of dancing in front of anything other than a mirror, you might find that the spirit of the event is enough to get you on the dance floor.

At your reception, your most important responsibility is to meet and greet each and every guest. Many of these people have traveled from a great distance at great expense to attend your wedding; the least you can do is say hello to them all. To do this, you have two options: the receiving line or table-hopping.

Outside of weddings, you haven't probably been to too many parties that featured receiving lines and may be unfamiliar with the practice. Like the name implies, a receiving line is simply a line of people who stand in a row *receiving* or greeting each guest. The most traditional receiving line, in order, consists of the mother of the bride, the mother of the groom, the bride, the groom, the maid of honor, and the bridesmaids. No men, except for the groom, appear in this traditional line. But do you really need to go this traditional? Probably not, as your family is probably not so formal that your aunts and uncles need to meet every member of your new wife's bridal party.

When couples do opt for the receiving line these days, they typically include the following people, in any variation of this order: the mother and father of the groom, the bride, the groom, and the mother and father of the bride. Variables such as divorced parents or who is paying for the wedding may influence the order you go with.

If you have a problem remembering names, a receiving line can be a great way to make up for that deficiency. Just position yourself immediately after your mother-in-law or bride and listen carefully as each guest comes up the line. You'll have a sneak preview before each person gets to you, and you can act as if you knew who they were all along.

The biggest advantage to a receiving line, of course, is that you will get to greet every single person who waits in line without having to move at all. Even if your guests are unfamiliar with the practice, they will soon figure out that if they want to guarantee some face time with you or your immediate family, they should get in line. Once the line is over, everyone can focus on the party.

They can do that, of course, if the line ever ends. Sixty guests at thirty seconds per guest will have you standing up shaking hands and kissing cheeks for only a half hour. But 250 guests at the same rate will result in a receiving line that lasts for over two hours. By the time you sit down, most of your guests will have moved on to dessert. Receiving lines may be traditional, but they are not always practical.

The solution that seems to fit most parties is for the bride and groom to table-hop. Hand in hand with your bride, you will walk from table to table, saying hello to everyone. This can take up a lot of energy, of course, as you'll be running around rather than letting the guests come to you, but going up to a table of ten people and saying hello to everyone at once is a lot easier than saying hello to each of those people individually. Besides, you'll have the rest of the party to socialize and can devote more individual attention to people as the party progresses. Another advantage to table-hopping? If you have any especially chatty guests, you can approach their table just as they are filling their mouths with chicken, making them unable to sustain any sort of long conversation.

SERIOUSLY, EAT SOMETHING— STAYING FUELED

I can't emphasize this advice enough. Your wedding day will find you riding high on a wave of adrenaline, but like a car down to its last few drops of gas, the risk of stalling runs high. From being on your feet for up to an hour during the ceremony to dancing with your bride, you'll expend a lot of energy on your wedding day. Staying properly fueled and hydrated is no less important for a groom than it is for a marathon runner.

Many couples take a few private moments to bask in the glow of their newlywed status after the ceremony, but when they show up at the cocktail party, they find that most of the hors d'oeuvres have already been eaten by hungry guests. Even if you arrive while supplies are running high, you may find yourself sidetracked by chatty guests eager to wish you and your new wife their hearty congratulations. A tray of food never seems farther away than when it is on the other side of your uncle Larry.

At a sit-down dinner, many couples make the rounds to all their guests during meal courses, since it's an easy way to find everyone to say hello. By the time the bride and groom get back to their table, however, their course of miso-glazed salmon and broccoli rabe, which they so eagerly anticipated, has made way for dessert. Talk to your caterer and have him or her instruct the waitstaff not to clear your plates until you have had a chance to eat.

If you are having a buffet at your reception, you'll probably be too busy to stand in line. Being the man of the hour entitles you to line-cutting privileges, so grab a plate and grab some food. You can also ask a friend to load up a plate for you and set it down at your table if you're otherwise occupied.

It's an ironic truth at countless weddings: after months of obsessing over menus and sampling food for your reception, you and your bride will probably be the two people least likely to enjoy any food at all on the big day. It certainly held true for Leora and me. Having barely had a moment to grab even a leaf of lettuce during our reception, the two of us stopped at a Burger King drive-through on our way back to our hotel and, dressed in our wedding best, consummated our marriage by eating Whoppers and onion rings.

DON'T DRINK AND JIVE—KNOWING YOUR LIMITS, EVEN AT A PARTY

Because you're likely to have little more than a few pigs in a blanket and a hastily eaten piece of cake in your stomach, drinking on your wedding day can be dangerous. Being tired and hungry are never good guards against getting drunk, so be mindful of your intake. Between organized champagne toasts and the sheer number of people who want to raise a glass with you on their own, you may find yourself offered countless glasses of alcohol. An open bar offers little incentive for your friends to lay off the sauce, but knowing when to say when can mean the difference between carrying your bride over the threshold into the honeymoon suite or being dragged there by hotel security.

MY TWO LEFT FEET—THE FIRST DANCE

Even if you're a budding Baryshnikov, getting up to dance with your bride for the first time can be nerve-racking. Is there any way to make sure your first dance goes off without a hitch? Short of channeling the spirit of Fred Astaire, probably not, but you can do some things to hone your hoofing skills.

The easiest step is to sign up for dancing lessons. Dance instructors would not be in business were it not for brides and grooms learning to fox-trot, Lindy, or swing, and with even a cursory Internet search or finger-walking trip through a telephone directory, you'll easily be able to find someone near you. Believe me, you won't be the first choreographically challenged guy to walk into a dance studio.

Whether you and your bride take lessons alone with an instructor or in a group setting, having a regular dance lesson helps in many ways. First and foremost, you'll learn how to do some basic dance moves that will help you build confidence for the moment when you and your bride step out into the spotlight. You'll also hold on to those skills for a long time and may even pick up a few moves to impress your friends and family at other people's weddings and events for years to come.

A huge residual but often-overlooked benefit to taking dance lessons is the time you and your fiancée spend together. This regular check-in can help you both take the focus off bigger wedding details.

For an extra bit of hand-holding, why not have your first dance choreographed by professionals? Emily Greenhill and Gabriella Barnstone are the founders of MatriMony Mony, a dance choreography service that has helped brides and grooms steal the show. After witnessing "too many painful, joyless first dances," Emily and Gabriella began mapping out moves for the soon-to-be-married. Just give them a copy of your song and they'll choreograph a dance that even the most rhythmically challenged bride and groom can follow. They'll teach you the moves and give you a videotape of your dance so you can practice at home. "Having someone else in charge of your dance moves is a good way to take the worry out of your wedding dance," says the dancing duo.

But don't think that you need to go to elaborate lengths just to avoid tripping over your bride's dress for three minutes. If all else fails, the most important skill when it comes to dancing is your own intelligence. Thinking quickly on your feet is sometimes more important than knowing how to move them, and when played with the right amount of humor and warmth, even the most Frankenstein-like of slow dancers can win the hearts of friends and family.

DANCE DANCE REVOLUTION— WHO DANCES WHEN?

You may have heard a lot about father-daughter and mother-son dances. Modern families can make such combinations more complicated than an all-black jigsaw puzzle, but let's start with tradition and go from there. Normally, people take to the dance floor in the following order:

- Bride and groom
- Bride's parents
- Groom's parents
- Bride and her father
- Groom and his mother-in-law
- Bride and her father-in-law
- Groom and his mother

After that, the bridal party and groomsmen join in and are soon followed by the rest of the guests. You and your bride might also want to have spotlight dances with grand-parents and siblings or could have to make special exceptions for stepparents, so feel free to shake things up when you're getting down. If each dance will be announced with an introduction, talk to your bandleader or DJ before your reception. Write the order on a sheet of paper and include it with any other information such as song lists that you give to whoever is in charge of providing music for your party.

Other traditional ethnic dances, such as a Jewish hora or Greek circle dance, may precede all of these dances. Your bandleader has probably seen hundreds of different cultural weddings, so check with him about when such a dance should take place.

DID YOU HEAR THE ONE ABOUT . . . ?— WEDDING TOASTS

In the most traditional of weddings, if your bride's family is the main sponsor of the day's proceedings, her father will most definitely make a toast, welcoming your guests to the party he has so generously paid for. Your mother-in-law might also say a few words. At celebrations where the hosting duties have been spread out over both families, it is also customary for one or both of your parents to say a few words.

Your best man, of course, may make a speech, and for many brides and grooms this is the most nail-biting event of the entire party. Halfway through his second course and, let's be honest, halfway through his fifth drink, your best man will get up to say a few words about you and your new wife. If your best man is a little toasted when he gives his toast, you might be worried about what will come out of his mouth. While you won't want to be too controlling by vetting his speech or censoring him, you can express your wishes that he be mindful of his audience.

Your best man should not catalog your past sexual exploits or tell stories about your nightmare ex-girlfriends. Your bride should come across as someone whom your friends see as the best woman in the world for you, not as the best after a long line of bad exes. You also don't want to be introduced to so many new family members as someone who has an incredible lack of judgment when it comes to romantic relationships.

Your fears, however, will probably be unfounded. If your best man is anything like you, he's probably thoughtful enough not to do anything to offend. In fact, even the most macho of your buddies might surprise you with his words and kind sentiments. Anyone who sees you at your happiest with a beautiful bride by your side will be moved by the experience, even if the only time anyone ever saw him cry was when Han Solo was frozen in carbonite at the end of *The Empire Strikes Back*.

The maid of honor might share the stage with your best man, and still other people might offer a few words, such as a grandparent, a sibling, or other close friends. But don't forget an equally important speaker: you. Public speaking is not necessarily something you usually have to do a lot of as a groom; normally you just say "I do" and leave it at that. But your ceremony is a perfect chance to offer thanks to the people who made your special day special. Offer toasts to your in-laws, your parents, your guests, and, most important, your bride.

If you're nervous about speaking in front of so many people, follow the age-old advice of starting with a joke to warm up the crowd. At my wedding I stood up and told people I had a quick announcement. "I just wanted to let you all know that from now on you can all call me by my married name," I said, "Mr. Douglas Gordon." I can't remember if the joke brought down the house, but it did ease my way into the rest of my speech.

LET US EAT CAKE— CAKE-CUTTING CEREMONIES

It's one of the most stereotypical images of thousands if not millions of weddings: during a cake-cutting ceremony, a bride and a groom share a piece of cake from a single plate, romantically linking arms and feeding each other. Then, in a burst of playfulness, the groom gently smashes a handful of frosting and cake into his bride's face. The bride then responds in kind, rubbing a fistful of icing into her new husband's smug smile. The crowd goes wild with laughter as the couple turns their cake-covered mugs toward the cameras for a few snapshots. The bride and groom kiss, pecking crumbs and icing from each other's lips and cheeks, so in love and happy with each other. But are they?

It may not usher in the first major fight of your marriage, but consider this: your bride, who probably spent a considerable amount of time and money having her makeup done before the ceremony, might not appreciate having her red lipstick smeared by a piece of red velvet cake. If you still have to pose for any pictures, your new wife probably won't want to do it while picking frosting out of her hair. An expensive wedding dress stained by chocolate might upset even the most levelheaded bride, even if all she had planned to do was store it in a closet for the rest of your lives.

Don't go into your cake-cutting ceremony assuming your bride wants a face full of frosting. You don't have to have a major discussion, but sometime before the reception ask her what she wants. While it may seem like a buzz killer to ask in advance about what seems like a moment of playful spontaneity, the fact that thousands of brides and grooms smash thousands of pieces of cake into each other's faces at thousands of weddings each year may undercut the idea of spontaneity to begin with.

You don't even necessarily have to have every part of your reception reduced to some sort of ceremony. Leora and I decided not to formally cut our cake, since doing so would instead cut into the time we'd be able to spend dancing the afternoon away with our friends. Instead, our cake was displayed for all our guests to see during the reception, then cut up by the caterer when it was time for dessert.

Be wary of event planners or bakers who try to sell you on expensive keepsake cake slicers. Spending hundreds of dollars on a cake cutter that few people will actually see up close for a ceremony that lasts only a few minutes is probably not a good use of your money, and it's a safe bet that the wedding-cake slicer an event planner tries to sell you is just a jazzed-up version of something anyone can buy at Target. Save the money and enjoy your cake.

SINGLED OUT—THE BOUQUET TOSS, GARTER TOSS, AND SINGLES TABLES

Among the most common events of most weddings are the bouquet toss and its traditional cousin, the garter toss. I believe it is time to put a stop to both practices once and for all.

Why? Let's look at the bouquet toss first, shall we? It's a superstition that the woman who catches the bride's bouquet will be the next to get married, but census data is unable to back up that claim. A bouquet toss might be okay if most of your friends are young, say under the age of twenty-five, and you are the first of your group to get married, but when you are in your late twenties or over the age of thirty and have only a handful of single friends remaining, why would you humiliate them in a desperate grab for a bunch of flowers? Making them wear a scarlet *A* on their chests for the entire reception would be no less cruel.

The garter toss, which begins with a groom reaching up his bride's dress to remove her stocking garter—usually with his teeth—and ends with him tossing it to a group of bachelors, is equally cringe-worthy, but for reasons that may have less to do with concern for others than with personal embarrassment. Do you really want to reach up your new wife's dress in front of her parents, your parents, grandparents, and everyone else you know? Don't you normally save that sort of thing for your bedroom or the backseat of your car? Pulling off your bride's garter is the wedding reception equivalent of walking down the street with your hand in the back pocket of her blue jeans. Don't do it.

Put together, I believe the bouquet and garter tosses are

unbelievable breaches of etiquette, taste, and decorum. Even more unbelievable is that these traditions usually live on at weddings where etiquette, taste, and decorum are otherwise of the highest importance. No matter how expensive a bridesmaid's dress, it will get dirty when she lands on the floor in a running dive for a bouquet of flowers. And whether he's wearing a traditional tuxedo or a white tie and tails, no groomsman looks classy when he's sniffing a woman's garter in front of her relatives.

Speaking of your single friends, many couples wonder where they should be seated, balancing a desire to play match-maker with the knowledge that some of these single friends might actually be closer with friends who are already coupled off. Weddings are, of course, great places to meet people, as coming together for the marriage of mutual friends is one thing your single guests will already have in common when they meet. But don't fall into the trap of exiling your single friends to Siberia by seating them all in the same place.

Just because you have ten single friends doesn't mean you have to sit them all at the same table. Why not seat six of those people at a table with two couples, and the other four bachelors and bachelorettes at a table with three cou-ples? Don't be one of those couples that get engaged and then suddenly are unable to divide by anything other than the number two. As an Engaged Groom, your math skills should be better than that.

If you must have a singles table or two, be creative. Steve, a banker from Seattle, tells of one nightmare scenario: "I sat at a singles table a few years ago. It was all guys! The couple didn't even do us the favor of sitting us next to avail-able women."

FOR THE BIRDS?—
RICE AND OTHER THINGS
YOUR GUESTS CAN THROW AT YOU

As you leave your ceremony and head down the steps of your church or through the parking lot toward your waiting limo, you may find yourself showered with everything from rice to confetti to candy. In many ancient cultures, including those of Egypt and Rome, throwing rice was considered a way to bestow blessings of fertility upon a newly married couple. While we may be more educated about sex and fertility than the ancient Egyptians and Romans were, the tradition of throwing things at newlyweds endures. It's quaint, somewhat pointless, but harmless. Or is it?

You may have heard that throwing rice at a couple as they leave the ceremony is no longer considered ecologically correct. For years, rumors have circulated that rice left on the ground after a wedding is harmful to birds. Like the fate that was rumored to have befallen Life cereal's Mikey, who allegedly died after mixing Pop Rocks and soda, birds are said to be in danger of having their stomachs explode when uncooked rice expands inside.

Planning our own wedding, Leora and I were a little skeptical of this claim. Have you ever been to a wedding where the church parking lot was littered with hundreds of dead pigeons? We hadn't really given much thought to what our guests would throw at us or if they would throw anything at all, although we had joked that wadded-up hundred-dollar bills would be nice. Like a premarital Hardy Boy, I decided to solve the mystery of the bird-killing rice.

The idea that rice expands inside the stomachs of birds, killing them from within, can be sourced to an old Ann Landers column. In the late eighties, the advice columnist advised her readers against the practice, citing the barbaric and sadistic harm done to avian ecology. The myth was further perpetuated on a morning TV talk show, when a wedding planner cautioned viewers about throwing rice. It even found its way into an episode of *The Simpsons*, with Bart taking special delight in the prospect of exploding birds, grabbing a bag of rice and a video camera, and running outside after his environmentally conscious sister, Lisa, warns Marge about the danger.

But one fact remains: *uncooked rice is not harmful to birds.* Rice farmers, in fact, probably wish that it were, as birds can be terrible liabilities to their livelihoods, eating up a valuable crop before it can be harvested. But even though everyone from ornithologists to the USA Rice Federation has written this story off as an urban legend, it still persists. Why?

Because the wedding industry wants to sell you some bubbles. Not just any bubbles, but bubbles in bottles shaped like hearts, flowers, champagne bottles, and even cowboy boots. While I would stop short of blaming ruthlessly powerful bubble lobbyists or a cabal of event planners, take anyone who tells you that you need to spend $40 on a case of bubble bottles with a grain of, well, rice. A $4 sack of Uncle Ben's might do the trick just fine.

That's not to say you might not prefer bubbles anyway. (Getting pelted in the eye with a grain of rice is a terrible way to start your honeymoon.) Some couples opt for rose petals, confetti, or other soft alternatives. Birdseed is another popular alternative, as it leaves a less unsightly mess than rice.

One wedding magazine I read suggested the release of doves after a wedding celebration since the birds are a beautiful symbol of peace. Right. Nothing says "peace" like buying a dozen birds from a pet store and keeping them in a cage for six hours during your wedding.

No matter what you choose, check with facility managers first. Birdseed might seem like a good idea to your family, but not to the country club manager who'll be helpless to prevent a flock of birds from feasting off his professionally manicured golf course. Some churches may even see rice as a legal liability. Thousands of tiny grains scattered around a polished marble floor can make walking dangerous for your less sure-footed wedding guests.

DON'T STOP THINKING ABOUT TOMORROW

So you did it. After all the budgeting, envelope licking, list making, and general planning, you are married. You probably feel a great sense of relief now that it's all over. The things that once consumed your every waking thought—whether to serve tilapia or salmon or which size frying pan to register for—now seem trivial in comparison to the enormous significance of your marriage. Now that there are no more events to plan, you want to throw your hands up in the air and exclaim, "Stick a fork in me, folks, I'm married."

Don't get too comfortable. There may still be bills to pay, and with gifts coming in for the next year, you may get writer's cramp just thinking about all the thank-you notes you'll have to write. You'll soon be sifting through stacks of pictures, deciding which to put in a wedding album. You may have to decide what to do with leftover food, favors, and invitations. No event is over when it's over, and the effects of your wedding day can linger for a long time. One couple I spoke with who accidentally ordered five thousand monogrammed paper napkins instead of five hundred will be wiping their mouths on their initials for years to come.

But even if you aren't going on a honeymoon right away, don't get mired down in the details. Take a well-deserved and much-needed break. (An ultimate wedding moratorium of sorts.) Pass the buck if need be or wait a week or two before you dive back into writing checks and dropping thank-you notes off at the post office. The day after your wedding is the first day of the rest of your married life, so relax. You deserve a break that day.

POSTPARTY DEPRESSION?— AFTER IT'S ALL OVER

Don't be surprised if a strange feeling washes over you and your new wife immediately after your wedding is over. It's perfectly normal and makes all the more sense when you consider the enormous significance of what you just experienced. For one day or even an entire weekend, you and your bride were surrounded by some of the most important people in your life. Your friends and family made you both the center of attention in a way you may not have been used to. Your party may have been an overload of sights and sounds that stimulated your senses like never before. But suddenly, the party is over. The guests all go home, the tables are cleared, and the confetti is swept from the dance floor. What remains are just two people: you and your new wife. After six months, a year, or more of planning, the biggest event of your lives so far is over in a matter of hours. As a result, the first few moments some couples spend alone together as husband and wife can feel a little lonely. Isn't it ironic?

But don't worry. You'll be back to your old selves again soon enough, ready to enjoy the sand, surf, and sun of a tropical honeymoon or the comforts of your new home together as Mr. and Mrs.

WORST SEX EVER

Busting the Myth of Wedding Night Sex

It might be a scene right out of a TV sitcom or a letter ripped from the pages of an adult magazine. A newly-wed couple rushes into their hotel suite, a young groom carrying his new wife over the threshold. They're full of vim and vigor and, of course, pent-up sexual energy. As the door to their room slams behind them, hotel guests in the hallway hear the new husband and wife in the throes of passion. The people in the neighboring room have a good chuckle listening to the couple's headboard slamming against the shared wall. The next morning the newlyweds exit their room with smiles running from ear to ear as they begin their honeymoon in earnest, the very picture of a gushing groom and a blushing bride indeed.

Even if you haven't saved yourself for marriage and have known your wife before the bonds of holy matrimony, the pressure to make your wedding night an earth-shattering, once-in-a-lifetime experience can be huge. Like other things couples are *supposed* to do, there is a commonly held belief that married couples always start things off with a bang.

Most newlyweds, however, have a not-so-dirty little secret. Ask anyone who was married recently and more than a few will tell you that the last thing they did was have sex the first night they spent together as husband and wife. Scratch that. It wasn't the last thing they did, because they didn't do it at all.

"We stayed up opening presents and totaling up the checks," says one anonymous groom. "By the end of it all we were too exhausted to move and went to bed."

For many couples the frenzy of the wedding day— the early-morning hours spent getting ready, an emotional ceremony, followed by energetic dancing and socializing, not to mention months of preparation and buildup—leaves them feeling spent by the time their wedding night rolls around. Sex, if it happens at all, is more textbook than storybook.

"A friend was joking at the reception that something like thirty percent of all brides and grooms don't do it on their wedding night, and he urged us not to be among the thirty percent," says Cris from Arlington, Virginia. "I think that is mostly why we did it at all, so we could say we weren't part of the thirty percent."

If your bride took on a lot of the wedding planning herself, she may be in no mood to respond to your wedding-night advances. So be sensitive. "Everybody does it" is probably the least romantic thing you can say to your new wife.

"Having sex on one's wedding night seems right up there with all the other wedding conventions that make no sense, like throwing garters," says Samara, a not-so-blushing bride from Takoma Park, Maryland. "I was up early, superstressed all day, went through the most emotional and meaningful moment of my entire life, and I'm supposed to suddenly have romantic feelings left over? Not me."

But lest you think Samara was holding out on her new hubby, the excitement and energy exhausted during a typical wedding day can leave even the most virile guy feeling exhausted.

"I think my husband was also worn-out," adds Samara. "He fell asleep pretty early and I was so wired I couldn't sleep until hours later. My memory of that evening was being very hungry, finding out the room service in the hotel had already ended, and sitting naked on the bed eating a can of Pringles I had fished out of the minibar. We didn't consummate things for three or four days later and that was just fine with us."

So if your wedding night leaves you and your bride feeling a little less than satisfied, you're not alone. According to Cris's statistic-spouting friend, 30 percent of all couples are just like you.

ONE OF LIFE'S CERTAINTIES

The Marriage Penalty

Despite that weddings are, on average, stupendously expensive, there are plenty of longtime financial advantages to getting married that may override your entire wedding budget. From sharing a health insurance plan to splitting the cable bill, married couples usually find that much of their living expenses are half that of their single friends.

You may have heard, however, that getting married brings with it a large tax burden, something commonly referred to as the marriage penalty, as if posing for a million photographs and having your cheeks pinched by your aunt Ida weren't punishment enough. Does the IRS really penalize people for getting married? Aren't politicians always railing about the sanctity of marriage?

You don't necessarily have to worry about getting hit with a huge tax bill come April 15. It all depends, of course, on how much you make. If you have an annual salary of, say, $50,000 and your wife does not work or makes only pocket money doing odd jobs here and there, you will probably see little change in your annual tax bill, as your wife's meager earnings won't bump you up into a higher tax bracket.

But let's be real. This isn't the 1950s and chances are better than not that your wife goes to an office every day just as you do. Your salaries are probably within striking distance of each other or your fiancée might even be the bigger breadwinner. Either way, get ready for a change. If you make $50,000 per year and your fiancée makes $50,000 per year, getting married will push you into a higher tax bracket, since you'll have a total household income of $100,000. Depending on your specific salaries, this can change your tax rate by 10 percent or more.

Don't take out your checkbook just yet. Much will affect your specific tax rate, including the number of deductions you take, mortgage payments, investment returns or losses, and contributions to retirement accounts. State and federal taxes vary wildly, and in some cases it might make more sense for you and your wife to continue filing separately. Congress and the White House continue to battle back and forth in an effort to reform the tax code, and with new formulas being written every year there's no telling exactly how much money you'll wind up owing Uncle Sam, if you wind up owing anything at all. Just remember that this is a book about wedding planning, not macroeconomics. As with any major financial matter, talk with a pro.

THE END AND THE BEGINNING

Getting married is an incredible experience. Being married is even better. Don't believe anyone who jokes about a ball and chain or the end of your freedom. While it might be too Hollywoodesque to say that your fiancée completes you, true partners bring out the best in each other. But you don't need a guidebook to tell you the secrets of a successful marriage, and that's certainly not why you're reading this one. You've probably picked up your own tricks of the trade along the way.

In fact, planning your wedding has probably brought your style as a couple into focus in ways that may at times have felt like an extreme close-up. You've probably had to make some of the biggest financial decisions of your life, while balancing the fragile egos of emotional family members and the personal tastes of people who may be as dissimilar as they are alike. You've had to make a thousand decisions, figuring out how much energy you wanted to invest in each one. You've had your fights, but you've also had your fun. No matter how involved you've gotten, the skills that have served you so well as an Engaged Groom will serve you even better as an Engaged Husband.

Some people spend so much time obsessing about tuxedos, flowers, and gift registries that they forget the true meaning of a wedding, like some sort of marital Scrooge. But not you. Not an Engaged Groom. No matter how big a production your wedding has been and how much of this is new to you, you've probably always kept your focus on the most certain part of getting married: a wedding lasts only a few hours, while a marriage is supposed to last a lifetime. There are no hard facts to support my theory, but I'd imagine that the people who spend tens of thousands of dollars on their wedding are no more or less likely to be happy on their thirtieth anniversary than the people who elope to city hall.

If you read this entire book, you may have noticed that not once did I use the term *cold feet*. Why not? Because being nervous before taking such a big step is normal. Not every late-night freak-out or pang of what-if means you are destined to a life of bachelorhood, eating franks 'n' beans from a can. Wondering about the future every now and then shows that you understand the commitment you're about to make. Heck, some people get nervous before signing a three-year lease on a car or taking a new job. That's not to say you should ignore any jitters or not talk about them with your fiancée. After all, she may feel exactly the same as you do.

But maybe it's not marriage that has you nervous, but the wedding. That's normal, too. Considering how nervous I was to hold hands with my prom date in high school when I picked her up at her parents' house, imagine how I felt kissing my new wife as over two hundred of our closest friends and family looked on.

So relax and have fun. Give yourself a pat on the back. You should be proud, as you are a rare breed of man. As an Engaged Groom, you've probably impressed a lot of people with your concern, participation, and sophistication. But don't be too impressed with yourself. So many guys are stepping up to help out with wedding planning these days that what you have done so far and will continue to do can hardly be considered help anymore. You are an equal participant, as eager to plan the biggest day of your life (so far) as your bride.

ELOPING—A QUICKIE GUIDE TO QUICKIE WEDDINGS

The classic image of eloping, as depicted in old Technicolor movies, is of a moonlit night in a quaint, suburban neighborhood. A girl of no more than eighteen lies in wait in her second-story bedroom for her beloved, whom her father sees as a no-good rebel without a clue. As her pompadoured lover pulls into the driveway in his shiny convertible, she stops brushing her hair and watches expectantly as he tips a ladder against an ivy-covered wall. Working quietly so as not to disturb the girl's parents, who are asleep in separate beds in the master bedroom, the fifties greaser carries his young bride down the ladder and puts her in his hot rod's passenger seat. The star-crossed lovers steal away into the night, living happily ever after as the credits roll.

Movie images like these are romantic, but hardly realistic. First of all, your bride-to-be probably doesn't live at home with her parents, and you may look less like James Dean and more like Jim Belushi. To top things off, there isn't a ladder long enough to reach your fiancée in her multistory apartment building.

Still, faced with the enormous effort and expense of planning a wedding, even the most progressive of Engaged Grooms might have moments when he wonders if it's worth it all. Wouldn't it be easier to just run down to city hall or catch the red-eye to Vegas? Here is a rank of some popular places for spur-of-the-moment nuptials, starting with the easiest:

Local city hall: Quick, cheap, and convenient, eloping to your town's city hall is a fast-acting solution to avoiding wedding headaches. Of course, if your bride's dad is the town sheriff, keeping your marriage a secret from nosy neighbors and your aunt Bee could be difficult. Especially if you live in Mayberry.

Las Vegas: Could there be a better place for eloping than the city that practically invented the quickie marriage? After a ceremony at Sin City's famous Little White Chapel for around $200 and the cost of a marriage license, you'll still have plenty of money left to play the slots. The only con? The Elvis impersonator's cape might clash with your bride's dress.

New York City: Despite a reputation for being an expensive city in which to live and play, making your relationship legal in New York is a great choice for bargain hunters, as inexpensive as the knockoff Rolexes and fake designer handbags for sale on Broadway. After you've spent $35 on a marriage license, you'll save a whopping $34,000 off the cost of the average Big Apple wedding ($33,954 if you factor in cab fare).

Mexico: Tying the knot south of the border is certainly convenient; your honeymoon can begin as soon as you kiss the bride. Toast your new marriage with as many margaritas as you like, but remember, don't drink the water.

Europe: After hopping a flight to Paris, Rome, or some
other romantic European location, you'll be free and
clear of meddling relatives. Just be careful to go to
the right government office when you're ready to
pledge your undying love to your bride. Given
potential language barriers and a reputation for
bureaucracy in some countries, you might wind up
pledging your undying support to a foreign
government instead.

Acknowledgments

Much of the anecdotes, advice, and opinions found in this book come from the online pages of PlanetGordon.com, a blog I kept to document my engagement year and wedding. I must offer my immense gratitude to the regular readers who made my humble site such a big success. Many of them are quoted in this book, and I thank them for their contributions. David Wadler, my unofficial technical consultant, also deserves special mention.

Additional thanks go to the friends and professionals who offered their help and advised me on some of the book's more important details: Gabriella Barnstone and Emily Greenhill, Rachel Kramer Bussel, Rabbi Matthew Gewirtz, Lori Leibovich and the entire community at IndieBride.com, Patrick Panico, Scott Patrick, Stuart Rosenberg, Laurie Shayler, and Jennifer Yoffe.

Matthew Benjamin, my editor at HarperCollins, gave me a lot of freedom with this book, which made my task of actually writing it a lot easier. Credit must be given where it is due, and after a long brainstorming session the idea for this book's title came from him.

Kate Lee, my fantastic agent at ICM, deserves many thanks for taking a chance and believing in my writing. She nurtured my book proposal and was with me every step of the way through its creation. Her faith, hard work, and easy-going nature will always be appreciated.

My parents, Neil and Sally, have always encouraged me and were the earliest fans of PlanetGordon.com. My sister, Becca, whose duties as my "best sister" began long before my wedding day, was a huge source of support.

As Leora and I planned our wedding, her parents, Jerry and Paula, were generous to a point where I eventually found it impossible to relate to other people's stories of meddling in-laws. I thank them, along with Alan and Michelle, for welcoming me into their family without hesitation.

The ultimate thanks and appreciation is reserved, of course, for Leora. Without her, I would never have been an Engaged Groom.

Index